Safeguarding Children Living with Foster Carers, Adopters and Special Guardians

Learning from case reviews 2007–2019

Hedy Cleaver and Wendy Rose

Published by
CoramBAAF Adoption and Fostering Academy
41 Brunswick Square
London WC1N 1AZ
www.corambaaf.org.uk

Coram Academy Limited, registered as a company limited by guarantee
in England and Wales number 9697712, part of the Coram group, charity
number 312278

British Library Cataloguing in Publication Data
A catalogue record for this book is available from the British Library

ISBN 978 1 910039 98 4

Project management by Jo Francis, Publications Department,
CoramBAAF
Designed and typeset by Helen Joubert Designs
Printed in Great Britain by The Lavenham Press

For the latest news on CoramBAAF titles and special offers, sign up to
our free publications bulletin at https://corambaaf.org.uk/subscribe.

Contents

Note about the authors

Dr Hedy Cleaver is an Emeritus Professor at Royal Holloway College, University of London. Her experience as a social worker and child psychologist informs her research on vulnerable children and their families and the impact of professional interventions. Most recently, she was part of the research team responsible for the last triennial review of serious case reviews (Brandon *et al*, 2020). The guiding principle underpinning her work is a desire to improve the quality of life for children living in circumstances that place them at risk of abuse and neglect. The findings from her research have had an identifiable impact on policy and practice in the UK in respect to children and families throughout the last 30 years.

Wendy Rose OBE held children's policy responsibilities at the Department of Health as Assistant Chief Inspector, following social work and senior management experience in the NHS and local authority. At the Open University as a Senior Research Fellow, she worked on research and development projects. During this time, she acted as a professional adviser to the Scottish Government on developing its children's policy, *Getting it Right for Every Child*. Latterly, she worked with the Welsh Government on its safeguarding reforms and as an Honorary Research Fellow at Cardiff University. She has published widely including, with Julie Barnes, the second biennial analysis of serious case reviews, *Improving Safeguarding Practice*, for the Department for Children, Schools and Families (2008).

Acknowledgements

This study has been a challenging and absorbing voyage of exploration. It initially involved us in finding and gaining access to the relevant case reviews, which was not quite as easy as we thought it would be. The findings then surprised us in a number of ways, and emphasised the importance of our focus on understanding what had happened to these children, and what the implications are for frontline practitioners and their managers, in an increasingly complex policy and practice environment.

We have been greatly helped and supported throughout the study. Jo Francis and her colleagues in CoramBAAF shared information with us on safeguarding reviews that they had received and they continued to do so during the year. We are indebted to Helen Walters and her team at the NSPCC Library for making us welcome and providing us with case reviews from their archives. They also took time to explain how the systems currently worked across the UK, their differences and the changes in hand. We had hoped to include cases from the four UK nations and had valuable discussions with Government safeguarding officials (Liz Pearce in Wales and Margaret Burke in Northern Ireland) and with academics who had undertaken overviews in Northern Ireland and Scotland (Professor John Devaney, Edinburgh University, and Dr Sharon Vincent, Northumbria University). We have built on the valuable work of Professor Marian Brandon and Professor Peter Sidebotham and appreciate their support and advice. Professor Judith Harwin has valiantly fielded our questions about special guardianship. We also wish to thank Dr Caroline Thomas, Barbara Firth and Professor Elaine Farmer, who encouraged us to undertake this study. Adrian Thompson gave us invaluable assistance at the final editing and proofreading stages. We thank those who read our final draft and the valuable comments they made. We are also grateful to Shaila Shah for her expertise in editing this publication. Finally, we wish to acknowledge the important work done in producing local safeguarding reviews that seek to provide dispassionate and constructive analysis of difficult and complex circumstances and bring about improvements in our services.

We are left with an abiding sense that children in our trust have not always been best served by the state and its services, and that there is still much to be learned and improved.

Chapter 1
Introduction

This study, commissioned by CoramBAAF, is the first to focus primarily on children who had been abused or neglected while living with foster carers, adopters or special guardians. This is a group of very vulnerable children for whom the state bears responsibility, as the corporate parent, for making arrangements for them to live safely and securely. What follows is an exploration of what happened to those who suffered serious harm or death and then became the subject of a local safeguarding review.

The study examines case reviews from across a dozen years (2007 to 2019) and identifies issues and themes that emerge. At the heart of the study is discussion about the pitfalls that were encountered and how professional culture, systems and practice in relation to these vulnerable children can be strengthened and improved. All this is set against the background of a very challenging environment for families and professionals in which to try and deliver care, support and a service that is always in the best interests of each child.

The findings are aimed particularly at practitioners and those managing and providing services for fostering, adoption and special guardianship, and members of fostering and adoption panels. The study has important messages for many disciplines, including child care social workers and supervising social workers, independent reviewing officers (IROs), and associated professionals in health, education, probation, police, immigration and court services. It is also relevant for a wider audience of those with responsibility for policy and practice in relation to safeguarding children.

The authors have written a companion guide to reflective practice that is intended to be read in conjunction with this study. This short guide discusses the key issues identified from the research and sets out a series of questions for practitioners based on the findings.

CONTEXT OF CHILDREN LIVING WITH FOSTER CARERS, ADOPTERS AND SPECIAL GUARDIANS

The last 30 years have seen an unprecedented growth in the numbers of children entering care in England and Wales. As a result, in 2017, local authorities in England and Wales 'had larger numbers of children in care than ever before' (Thomas, 2018, p.15). The inevitable pressures on existing local authority resources to meet the care needs of these children have been compounded in the last decade by a range of interrelated socio-economic factors. These factors include increasing levels of child poverty and family homelessness, at the same time as the implementation of Government fiscal policies of austerity and cuts in public services. The Select Committee examining the funding of local authorities' children's services in 2019 concluded:

> *Financial restraint combined with seemingly ever increasing demands on the sector is leading to what has been described as "a perfect storm".*

> (House of Commons Housing, Communities and Local Government Committee, 2019, p.3)

As at 31 March 2019, the number of children looked after in England was 78,150 (Department for Education (DfE), 2019a), three-quarters of whom were being cared for by foster families (Lawson and Cann, 2019). The steady rise in numbers has put enormous pressure on the supply and availability of foster carers, and on fostering services. Most placements are arranged through and overseen by local authorities themselves (Ofsted, 2020). During 2019, the number of local authority foster households in England remained static. In contrast, there has been a two per cent increase in the number of approved foster households provided by the independent sector (Ofsted, 2020). However, the latest data suggest that there continue to be 'fewer places available for children who needed foster care than in previous years' (Ofsted, 2020).

The situation has been exacerbated as a result of the coronavirus pandemic. From 1 March to 23 April 2020, the number of referrals to Barnardo's fostering services increased by 44 per cent while the number of people looking to become foster parents for the charity fell by 47 per cent compared with the same period in 2019. They report that:

> *... this has created a "state of emergency" as children who may have experienced abuse and neglect wait for places with loving foster families. Without more potential foster carers coming forward, hundreds of children referred to Barnardo's will not be placed with a family.*

> (Barnardo's, 2020)

A key Government policy has been to ensure that children in care experience family life that gives them security and permanence as they grow up. There has been considerable pressure on local authorities in England to increase each year the numbers of adoptions of children in the care system. This has had a measure of success. However, the number of looked after children in England who leave local authority care as a result of adoption has fallen by one-third in the past four years. A total of 3,570 looked after children were adopted in the year ending 31

March 2019. This contrasts with an increase in the numbers of children who left care through a special guardianship order, an outcome for 3,830 looked after children during the same period (DfE, 2019a). The DfE is urging a renewed focus on adoption as a permanence option (DfE, 2020a).

Not all placements proceed as planned. In 2018–2019, 5,815 children and young people in foster care (7%) were reported as having experienced unplanned endings of their placements, of whom 31 per cent were moved within 24 hours (Ofsted, 2020). There are no national statistics available for adoption disruption, but estimates are that between four and ten per cent of adoptions fail after the adoption order has been made (Selwyn *et al*, 2015). A disruption rate for special guardianship placements over a five-year period has been calculated at five per cent (Simmonds *et al*, 2019, p.12).

Placement disruption is an under-researched, complex area, and any statistics need careful examination and explanation (Selwyn *et al*, 2015). There is currently little evidence of an association between abuse and neglect of children living with foster carers, adopters or special guardians and placement disruption (Biehal *et al*, 2014).

IMPACT OF FUNDING CUTS ON CHILDREN'S SERVICES

As a result of the Government's austerity policies, local authority spending in recent years has not kept pace with demands for children's services (Thomas, 2018, p.32). A shortfall in children's social care funding was calculated by the Association of Directors of Children's Services (ADCS) and the Local Government Association (LGA) to be £2 billion (Thomas, 2018, p.63). The consequences of this were recognised by the Select Committee in 2019:

It is clear that current funding levels are unsustainable. Local authorities are responding to increasing demand and decreasing spending power by prioritising child protection work and reducing spending on non-statutory children's services. Despite these efforts, most local authorities are still overspending their budgets on children's social care.

(House of Commons Housing, Communities and Local Government Committee, 2019, p.3)

Alongside local authorities' limited and diminishing resources, there is evidence of increased use of private providers (Ofsted, 2020). Ray Jones (2019) has expressed concern that, in the private sector, the interests of shareholders or the owners of provider agencies can become as important as the quality of services provided. He suggests that this unrecognised growth in private for-profit provision within children's social care, including foster care services, raises worrying questions, not least the escalating costs to the purchasing local authorities.

PRESSURES ON THE SOCIAL WORK WORKFORCE

To work effectively to promote the well-being and safety of looked after children depends on there being sufficient, competent and caring social workers who are able to access and be supported by expert line management. This generally-held principle is currently being undermined by a number of factors, including difficulties in workforce recruitment and retention, pressures of practitioners' caseloads, and the culture of media and political "blame and shame" in which practitioners may find themselves working.

The Department for Education's (2020b) official statistics show that, for the period ending September 2019, vacancies stood at 16.4 per cent of the total children and families' social work workforce in England. The difficulties in recruiting permanent staff have resulted in an increasing dependence on private social work employment agencies. This has had an impact on the stability and quality of the children's workforce, and on local authorities' budgets, as employing agency staff inevitably results in higher costs than permanent staff:

> As of September last year, 26 authorities got more than 30 per cent of their children's social work staff from agencies.

(Perraudin, 2019)

The size of social workers' caseloads is another issue. There appears to be a "postcode lottery" in relation to both caseloads and unfilled vacancies (DfE, 2020b). The average caseload carried by children and family social workers in 2019 was 17.4 cases, but varied greatly between local authorities, from 12.1 cases in one authority to 32.7 in another. Vacancy rates also differed, being highest in London, with 24 per cent unfilled vacancies (DfE, 2020b). A theme from submissions to the Care Crisis Review was concern about the increasing complexity of cases and the challenge this created in terms of planning and service provision (Thomas, 2018). Many social workers report that their professional ethic of helping is undermined 'because of a lack of early help and support services available, the rising nature of thresholds and the lack of time to spend with families' (Frost, 2019).

A further strand is the wider environment, which has seen 'a growth in the culture of blame and an increased need for scapegoats' (Dingwall and Hillier, 2015, p.x). Social workers are all too aware that they may face media and political criticism and have an ever-increasing fear of getting things wrong. The Care Crisis Review reported:

A recurring theme in contributions to [care crisis] Review meetings and in written submissions about policy and practice was about an increasingly risk-averse and blame culture that pervades public work. The Review was told that fear of being vilified publicly and judged to have failed to prevent a child's injury or death haunts many professionals.

(Care Crisis Review, 2018, p.24, para 3.13)

The issue of blame and shame is an important contributory factor in local authorities' ability to retain their workforce. A diminished workforce, together with the turnover of staff and high caseloads, will inevitably impact on the quality of work carried out by children and family social workers.

A feature of the 52 case reviews studied was that there was no evidence of seeking to blame or shame individual staff, but the emphasis was on learning and improvement of professional culture, systems and practice.

SOURCES OF EVIDENCE ABOUT MALTREATMENT OF CHILDREN IN CARE

To ensure that the findings of this Good Practice Guide build on previous work on children who have been harmed or killed while living with alternative carers, other sources of information have been sought and examined. This was done in order to cross-check the findings from this guide and to gain a sense of the scale and extent of abuse by foster carers, adopters and special guardians. The search has revealed limited evidence, other than from serious case reviews, on the extent of abuse in foster care, adoption or special guardianship (Biehal *et al*, 2014).

Earlier public inquiries and reviews have been influential in shaping public and professional understanding of what happens when children, living in the care of others, are maltreated. They have also had an important role in informing subsequent legislative change.

The Home Office inquiry (conducted by Sir Walter Monckton) in 1945 into the death of Dennis O'Neill was the first to examine in detail the circumstances of what happened to a child and his brother in foster care (Cmd. 6636, 1945). A far-ranging Government Care of Children Committee had already been set up and reported in 1946. It was charged with enquiring into:

...existing methods of providing for children who from loss of parents or from any cause whatever are deprived of a normal home life with their own parents or relatives; and to consider what further measures should

be taken to ensure that these children are brought up under conditions best calculated to compensate them for the lack of parental care.

(Cmd. 6922, 1946)

The Committee's recommendations for the closer supervision of foster homes and their careful selection were clearly influenced by the death of Dennis O'Neill, and subsequently incorporated into the significant post-war legislation, the Children Act 1948 (Parker, 1999).

When Peter Reder and colleagues, some 40 years later, came to study 35 fatal child abuse inquiry reports from 1973 to 1989, they found many of the children in their study had been 'temporarily placed outside the household with extended family, previous partners or in the care of social services' at the time they died. Four of the children concerned had been in foster care or adoptive families (Reder *et al*, 1993, p.35). Their study broke new ground, and the insights into the "family-professional systems" and "professional networks" continue to be valuable and relevant, and are mirrored by findings in this study (see Chapter 6).

A scrutiny of biennial and triennial reviews of serious case reviews in England also informed the context of this study. These highlighted, for example, the vulnerability of older children and those with additional needs, such as disabled children, posing challenges for effective service provision (Rose and Barnes, 2008; Sidebotham *et al*, 2016). Other reviews drew attention to overwhelming caseloads, lack of professional confidence and insufficient qualified staff, uncertainty about information sharing, and the lack of rigour in assessment, analysis and plans (Brandon *et al*, 2009; Sidebotham *et al*, 2016). Most recently, the work of Marian Brandon and colleagues (2020) highlighted, among other important messages, the fragmentation of services, the need for clear multi-agency plans, and the importance of thorough assessments, suitable monitoring and support for children living with special guardians.

Finally, court judgements provided valuable insights through their detailed analyses of complex issues. Two, in particular, raised issues about the consequences of institutional failures on the lives of children. One related to two unconnected young people, where Mr Justice Keehan highlighted the impact on children's welfare of the inappropriate use of accommodation under s.20 of the Children Act 1989. The foster carers of both children were highly commended, but the local authority was severely criticised for failing to act in the best interests of the children. The judge commented that these were the 'most egregious abuses of section 20 accommodation it has yet been my misfortune to encounter as a judge' (*Family Law Week*, 2018).

The other court judgement, made by Mr Justice Jackson, highlighted the consequences of failing to revoke freeing orders on two brothers once the plan for adoption had been abandoned. As a result, 'in the ten years since the making of the order, the boys had no natural person with parental responsibility for them' (*Family Law Week*, 2012). The local authority action in relation to these two boys was seen to have been unlawful, as it breached their 'right to respect for private and family life'.

Over a 14 year period, A and S were moved from one foster family to another, becoming increasingly unsettled and disturbed. A had moved backwards and forwards between placements 77 times in his 16 years of life, and S had moved 96 times in his 14 years of life. The boys suffered physical and sexual abuse while in foster care.

(Chesterfield, 2012)

AIMS OF THIS STUDY

This study focuses on serious case reviews undertaken between 2007 and 2019 and which related to children living with foster carers, adopters or special guardians. A broad interpretation of what constituted a "serious case review" was taken. It encompassed a wide range of safeguarding practice reviews commissioned by Local Safeguarding Children Boards and included an Independent Inquiry following criminal proceedings.

The aim was to identify key issues, themes and challenges for practitioners and their agencies, working singly and collectively, and to draw out the learning for policy and practice.

The criteria for inclusion in the sample were:

- reviews published from January 2007 to July 2019;

- cases of serious harm and child death while living with foster carers, adopters or special guardians;

- wherever possible, cases to be drawn from the four nations: England, Wales, Northern Ireland and Scotland.

Accessing reviews

A variety of sources was used to identify reviews, including the NSPCC website and its archives, a search of relevant literature, and contact with key Government officials and academics in Wales, Scotland and Northern Ireland. At the time of the study, all nations had either reformed or were in the process of reviewing their systems for serious case reviews (or the equivalent).

The Working Together guidance 2018 for England introduced a new framework of child safeguarding practice reviews that changed the criteria for triggering a review from the previous guidance in 2015 (HM

Government, 2018). It established new working arrangements, replacing local safeguarding children boards with safeguarding partners and introduced the Child Safeguarding Practice Review Panel to oversee the operation of local and national safeguarding reviews (HM Government, 2018; NSPCC, 2019). The arrangements for publication were confirmed:

Safeguarding partners must publish local reviews and the panel must publish national reviews, unless they consider it inappropriate to publish.

(NSPCC, 2019)

It soon became clear that it would not be possible to include findings from Northern Ireland in this study. The Safeguarding Board for Northern Ireland is responsible for deciding whether an executive summary of a Case Management Review should be published. Periodic reviews that focus on specific issues, and include children living with foster carers, have been published and have been explored (see for example, Devaney *et al*, 2012; 2013). Only two executive summaries had been published in Northern Ireland since 2012, neither of which met the criteria for this study.

Including the findings from Significant Case Reviews (SCR) from Scotland also proved difficult because, once a review is completed, it is the responsibility of the child protection committee to decide whether to publish the full report or just an executive summary. Since 2012, the Care Inspectorate in Scotland has become the 'central collation point and undertakes qualitative evaluation on all significant case reviews' (Care Inspectorate, 2019, p.1). Overviews of SCRs have been periodically commissioned in Scotland and relevant ones have been scrutinised (Vincent, 2010; Vincent and Petch, 2012), as have the Care Inspectorate's more recent overviews of SCRs (Care Inspectorate, 2013; 2016; 2019).

At the time of publication, Serious Case Reviews (England), Child Practice Reviews (Wales) and Significant Case Reviews (Scotland) were being sent to the NSPCC by the respective Safeguarding Board or Partnership and made available through the NSPCC website for three years. They were thereafter stored in the NSPCC archives. However, discussions with the Head of Knowledge and the Senior Information Specialist responsible for the NSPCC repository painted a less certain picture. Although Local Safeguarding Children Board websites are routinely scanned for any missing reviews, the NSPCC could not be certain that all reviews had been identified and included in its repository. Staff had also noted an increase in requests to the NSPCC for publication of reviews to be anonymous.

METHODS OF ANALYSING THE DATA

A search was made of the NSPCC national case review repository and the websites of individual Local Safeguarding Children Boards to locate as many published reports of serious case reviews, and their equivalents, as possible for inclusion in this study.

A total of 52 completed reviews were obtained by the end of July 2019. These included:

- English Serious Case Reviews = 45 (4 of which concerned unnamed local authorities);

- Welsh Serious Case Reviews and latterly, since 2013, Child Practice Reviews = 6;

- Scottish Significant Case Reviews = 1.

We have used "serious case reviews" as a generic term for the 52 reviews in the study and often use the term "review" to avoid repetitiveness.

A mixed-methods approach was used to analyse the data. This included a quantitative and qualitative analysis of the full sample of 52 serious case reviews or their equivalent. Such an approach provides much information from which to draw out the implications for policy and practice.

An initial scrutiny of the reviews showed that no consistent approach had been taken to conducting the review. The methods varied, and included those described as:

- multi-agency deep dive review (refers to the extensive use of multi-agency chronological data);

- hybrid systems methodology (focuses on both continuous time variables and discrete events);

- blended methodology (a conscious mix of research methods to exploit their strengths and weaknesses);

- Appreciative Inquiry (a management approach that focuses on strengths rather than weaknesses to identify what is working well and why, in order to improve practice).

There were also significant differences in the form of the reviews. In some cases, a full review was available. These varied in the detail they gave and ranged from 27 to more than 80 pages. In other cases, only a brief summary report was obtainable. A few reviews had been redacted, in some cases making them unreadable and incomprehensible. Others had been published anonymously, and had redacted the identity of the local authority and the safeguarding board.

The reviews also varied in the extent of the information they provided about the child and family. For example, in a number of them, information on the child's age, gender, disability and ethnicity was not recorded. The inclusion of a genogram was not routine, making it difficult to make sense of often very complex family relationships. These omissions, although impacting on the veracity of the research, are understandable in the context of preserving the privacy of the child or birth family.

The timeframe was a publication date of the review between January 2007 and July 2019. This meant that in some cases the recruitment of carers and the placement of children had occurred under legislation, policy and practice of the 1970s, 1980s and 1990s. Although major changes in legislation have taken place since the 1970s (see, for example, Lord and Cullen, 2016, in relation to adoption legislation and guidance since 1989), similar themes emerged from the reviews, regardless of whether they were historic or more recent cases.

To compare the sample in the current study with that included in the triennial review of serious case reviews 2014–2017 (Brandon *et al*, 2020), the same details were extracted. This information was coded onto a Microsoft Excel spreadsheet for analysis, and included:

- demographic characteristics (region, residence, age, gender, ethnicity, disability prior to incident);
- category of death or serious harm;
- source of harm/perpetrator;
- social care involvement.

In addition, because the study focused specifically on cases involving children living with foster carers, adopters or special guardians, understanding the process and quality of the assessment and approval of carers was an important issue.

All 52 reviews were also subjected to a qualitative analysis where the focus was on the individual child or children. The analysis involved inductive, open coding. This meant that the reviews were read and re-read in order to identify themes, patterns and relationships common to the reviews. These were compared with data from relevant literature. The findings are illustrated with quotations (presented in italics) drawn from the serious case reviews and reproduced from the orginal. The results from the qualitative analysis provided insights into and an understanding of how and why these tragedies occurred.

Chapter 2
The findings from the 52 serious case reviews

This chapter provides the findings from a quantitative analysis of the 52 serious case reviews, or the equivalent, that relate to the serious harm or death of a child living with foster carers, adopters or special guardians. The number of children in the sample was 98 and the reviews spanned a 12-year period from 2007 to 2019.

The first part analyses the data about the children, their ages, and types of placement, and the assessment of potential carers. Where possible and relevant, comparisons are made with the findings from the most recent triennial review of 368 serious case reviews between 2014 and 2017 (Brandon *et al*, 2020). There are some caveats: the triennial study covered cases of child deaths and serious harm in England that resulted in a serious case review over a three-year period – only 16 per cent of cases were of children who were or had been looked after. However, the current study focuses on serious harm and child deaths in cases where children were living in alternative care situations in England (the majority), Wales and Scotland and covers a 12-year period. Nevertheless, some of the similarities and differences are of interest but any extrapolations from comparing the two datasets should be done with some caution. The small number of reviews included in this study makes any analysis of the data, in terms of distribution across English regions or between the nations in the UK, untenable.

The second part explores the data in respect of the 98 children to provide a more nuanced picture.

PART 1: SIMILARITIES AND DIFFERENCES WITH FINDINGS OF THE 2020 TRIENNIAL REVIEW

Many of the reviews concerning children who had died or suffered serious harm featured more than one child. The 52 reviews included in this study relate to 98 children. This issue was also identified in earlier triennial reviews, although at a lower incidence. For example, 16 (31%) reviews in the current study related to more than one child, whereas this was noted in only 22 (6%) of the 368 reviews in the triennial analysis (Brandon *et al*, 2020).

Table 1: Serious case reviews involving more than one child (n=16)

Number of reviews	Number of children included in the review
1	8
1	7
2	5
5	4
3	3
4	2
Total = 16	Total = 62

Reason for the serious case review

The 52 reviews in the study include 19 (37%) cases where a child had died and 33 (63%) where one or more children had suffered serious harm. This is a different and contrasting balance than was found in the most recent triennial analysis of data, which provides information for a similar period, 2005 to 2017, (Brandon *et al*, 2020, p.30, Table1). Their findings show that child deaths accounted for 62 per cent and serious harm for 38 per cent of serious case reviews over this timeframe. Only 16 per cent of cases concerned children who were looked after or previously looked after.

Identifying an index child

To compare the current findings with the triennial data, where the analysis focuses on an index child, a typical, specific child (index child) was identified when reviews related to numerous children.

Age of index child

Not all the serious case reviews recorded the age of the children. In five reviews, age was not reported, resulting in information being available for only 47 of the possible 52 identified index children.

Table 2: Age of index child

Age of child	Current study (n=47)		Triennial analysis (n=368)	
←1 year	9	19%	154	42%
1–5	8	17%	79	21%
6–10	10	21%	20	5%
11–15	14	30%	63	17%
16+	6	13%	52	14%

Table 2 compares the age grouping of children in this study with those included in the triennial analysis, and shows real differences. Children who had died or suffered significant harm in this study tended to be in middle or late childhood: over half (51%) were between the ages of 6 and 15 years, compared with 22 per cent in the triennial analysis. In contrast, children included in the triennial analysis (Brandon *et al*, 2020) tended to be young; 63 per cent were aged five years or younger, compared with 36 per cent in the current study.

Type of placement

The criteria for inclusion in this study were cases in which children had been living with foster carers, adopters or special guardians at the time of the incident. Also included were the data from two Welsh Child Practice Reviews of cases of a child living with a neighbour under a residence order. In both cases, the placement had started as a fostering arrangement and as a result, for this analysis, these have been incorporated into the group "living with foster families". A scrutiny of all the reviews shows that the majority related to children living in foster placements.

Table 3: Type of placement at time of harm or fatality

Placement	Death	Serious harm	Total	
Foster family	15	24	39	75%
Adoptive family	2	5	7	13%
Special guardianship	2	4	6	12%
Total	**19**	**33**	**52**	**100%**

Involvement of children's social care at time of harm or fatality

A scrutiny of the reviews shows that children's social care was not working with the family at the time of the incident in 10 cases, which comprised:

- four special guardianship placements;

- three adoption placements;

- two under residence orders; and

- one private fostering arrangement.

In four of the 10 placements where children's social care was not involved, the child had died.

Assessment of potential carers

The assessment and approval of prospective carers is the responsibility of fostering services and adoption agencies. It is essential to the safety and welfare of the children who will be placed with them that the assessment is carried out fastidiously and that all information is cross-checked. A scrutiny of the data suggests that this was not always the case; the reviews identified concerns in the assessment of potential carers in 23 of the 52 serious case reviews.

Table 4: Assessment of potential carers: concerns

Potential carer	No concerns		Concerns		Total number of reviews
Foster carer	25	64%	14	36%	39
Adopters	4	57%	3	43%	7
Special guardian	0	0%	6	100%	6
Total	**29**	**58%**	**23**	**42%**	**52**

Table 4 shows that concerns were identified in 14 (36%) of the reviews involving foster carers and in 3 (43%) of those involving adopters. Concerns over the quality of the assessments were identified in the review of all of the six special guardians included in the sample, an issue also identified by Brandon and colleagues in the triennial analysis of serious case reviews (Brandon *et al*, 2020).

An exploration of whether identified concerns relating to the assessments of prospective carers were associated with the type of abuse perpetrated is shown in Table 5.

Table 5: Review findings of assessment concerns and abuse perpetrated

Quality of assessment	Fatality		Sexual abuse		Physical abuse		Neglect		Other	
No concerns	14	74%	66	38%	6	46%	1	50%	2	100%
Concerns	5	26%	10	62%	7	54%	1	50%	0	0%
Total	19	100%	76	100%	13	100%	2	100%	2	100%

Although the numbers are small, the data suggest a higher death rate in cases where the reviews had not identified concerns with the quality of the assessment. However, this is misleading because in eight of these 14 cases the children had intentionally or unintentionally killed themselves. Perhaps of more relevance is the finding that the reviews identified concerns with the assessments of potential carers in a slightly greater proportion of cases where carers had sexually abused the children in their care, than for carers perpetrating other types of abuse.

PART 2: THE 98 CHILDREN – WHO ARE THEY AND WHAT HAPPENED TO THEM?

The previous section used an index child to identify similarities and differences with the much larger English sample of serious case reviews included in the latest triennial analysis (Brandon *et al*, 2020). What follows is an exploration of the data as they relate to the 98 children who were identified in the 52 serious case reviews covered in this guide. Focusing on individual children provides a greater understanding of the circumstances and characteristics of those who had been seriously harmed. In doing so, it reveals more relevant information for professionals working to protect children in foster, adoptive or special guardianship placements.

The serious case reviews included in this study relate to a slightly higher proportion of girls (n=49, 54%) than boys (n=41, 46%) (the gender of the child was not recorded in eight cases). This contrasts with Government statistics (Ofsted, 2018) that showed that 56 per cent of looked after children were male and 44 per cent female (consistent over the last four years). However, it would be unsafe to draw any conclusions from the small difference in the numbers.

Other personal information about the children was not always available from the reviews. For example, the ethnicity of the child was rarely recorded if the child was not from a minority ethnic group. The data are, therefore, unreliable because where information is missing it cannot be assumed that the children were White British. However, it is likely that they would be so classified, because recent Government statistics show that white children accounted for 76 per cent of all fostered children; 23 per cent belonged to non-white, minority ethnic groups; and the remaining one per cent to an unknown ethnic group (data and terminology as provided in Ofsted, 2020). Ethnicity had been recorded in the reviews included in this study for 23 children: five were White British, 12 were from Black or Black British families, four were of dual heritage, one child was Asian, and one Chinese. References in the text to a child's ethnicity use the terminology recorded in the relevant serious case review.

Child deaths

Nineteen children had died; half (n=8) of the children had intentionally killed themselves or died through a drug overdose.

Table 6: How children died

Category of death	Number of deaths
Fatal physical abuse	7
Suicide	7
Extreme neglect	1
Overt filicide	1
Poisoning (drug overdose)	1
SUDI (sudden unexplained death)	1
Other	1
Total	**19**

Child's age at time of death

How children died was related to their age. As would be expected, children who had taken their own lives tended to be older: three were aged between 11–15 years, and four were 16 years or older. In contrast, younger children were more vulnerable to fatal physical abuse: three were under a year old, two were aged between 1–5 years, one was of primary school age, and one was aged between 11–15 years.

Table 7: Age of children who had died

Child's age	Number of children
←1	4
1–5	4
6–10	2
11–15	5
16+	4
Total	**19**

Gender of children who had died

In all but one of the 19 reviews of a child death, the gender of the child was recorded. These 18 children included equal numbers of girls and boys. Although the group is very small and any extrapolation would be unsafe; nonetheless, it is interesting to note that there was no apparent relationship between the gender of a child and how he or she had died; for example, four girls and three boys had committed suicide.

Mental health of children who had died

A focus on the seven children who had committed suicide and the one who had died from self-administered drugs shows that three had identified mental health issues and two had serious drug and alcohol problems, prior to killing themselves.

Child's placement when fatality occurred

An examination of where the 19 children had been living when they died shows that 15 were with foster carers, two with adopters and two with special guardians. This bias is to be expected, and reflects the far greater number of children placed in foster care than adopted or living with special guardians (DfE, 2018a).

Children who had suffered serious harm

The 33 serious case reviews where a child had experienced serious harm related to 79 children. Table 8 shows that nearly two-thirds (62%) of the children had been sexually abused by their carers, with a much smaller proportion having experienced physical harm or neglect (34%). The category of serious harm for three children had been classified as "Other". These three children had suffered abuse and neglect prior to coming into care, but the review was triggered by and focused on the serious harm or fatality caused *by* the child. The cases include: a 13-year-old girl who, along with another similarly aged girl, had stabbed and killed a vulnerable woman; a 15-year-old boy with special educational needs who had sexually abused other boys in the same foster home; and a 13-year-old boy who had stabbed to death his foster mother.

Table 8: Category of serious harm

Category of serious harm	Number of children (%)	
Sexual harm	49	(62%)
Physical harm	23	(29%)
Severe neglect	4	(5%)
Other	3	(4%)
Total	**79**	**(100%)**

Gender of children who suffered serious harm

Of the 79 children featured in reviews relating to serious harm, the gender of 72 children was reported. Within this group, there was a predominance of girls: 40 girls and 32 boys. Table 9 shows the relationship between the type of serious harm the children had experienced and their gender.

Table 9: Gender of the child and category of serious harm experienced

Gender	Sexual	Physical	Severe neglect	Other	Total
Girls	30	9	0	1	40
Boys	18	10	2	2	32
Total	**48**	**19**	**2**	**3**	**72**

Sexual abuse was the most prevalent form of serious harm, and girls were particularly vulnerable, being the victims of nearly two-thirds (62%) of the sexual harm perpetrated. In contrast, equal numbers of boys and girls had been physically harmed while in the care of foster carers, adopters or special guardians.

Age of children who suffered serious harm

Of the 79 children who had experienced serious harm, the age of the child at the time the serious case review was conducted was recorded for 58 children. The recorded age does not necessarily reflect the age of the child when the abuse first occurred, and caution must be taken in any extrapolation from these data. Some children did not speak of the harm they had experienced until they had reached adulthood.

Table 10: Age of child and category of serious harm experienced

Age	Sexual	Physical	Severe neglect	Other	Total
←1	0	4	1	0	5
1–5	6	3	0	0	9
6–10	18	1	1	0	20
11–15	8	6	1	3	18
16+	2	4	0	0	6
Total	**34**	**18**	**3**	**3**	**58**

Table 10 supports the earlier finding that focused on an index child for each serious case review. The majority of the children who had been victims of all forms of serious harm were in middle or late childhood; two-thirds were between the ages of 6 and 15 years when the abuse became known. The data show that the most prevalent form of harm was sexual abuse by the children's carers, and pre-pubescent children were particularly vulnerable; 18 children (53%) were between the ages of 6–10 years, and six were no more than five years old when the abuse was identified as having taken place.

Child's placement when serious harm occurred

An exploration of the data in terms of individual children who had suffered serious harm highlights the complexity of some households. For example, a family who were registered foster carers already had three older children living with them on residence orders at the time the local authority placed two foster children. Similarly, a woman who had adopted two children had a sibling group of three living with her on residence orders. As a result, Table 11 includes the category of residence order, and breaks down the data accordingly.

The majority of the serious case reviews featured foster care placements (see Table 3). An analysis of the reviews in terms of individual children showed similar results; the majority (70%) of children were living with foster carers.

Table 11: Placement where children experienced serious harm

Placement	Sexual harm		Physical harm		Severe neglect		Other		Total	
Foster care	40	(73%)	9	(16%)	3	(5%)	3	(5%)	55	(70%)
Adoption	1	(11%)	7	(78%)	1	(11%)	0		9	(11%)
Special guardianship	4	(50%)	4	(50%)	0		0		8	(10%)
Residence order	4	(57%)	3	(43%)	0		0		7	(9%)
Total	**49**	**(62%)**	**23**	**(29%)**	**4**	**(5%)**	**3**	**(4%)**	**79**	**(100%)**

Serial sexual abuse

Half of the serious case reviews concerning serious harm related to more than one child in that household. Sixteen serious case reviews related to the sexual abuse of a child, of which nine (56%) involved multiple children; for example, one review featured seven young boys, and in another, a male foster carer had sexually abused eight girls. In the majority of cases involving the sexual abuse of multiple children, the perpetrator was an adult male; in one case, the perpetrator was a resident male foster child.

Of considerable concern is the finding that, on more than one occasion, the review uncovered additional children who had been harmed. In three of the nine reviews involving a serial sex abuser, children (related and unrelated) not known to children's social care had also been sexually abused. For example, one review noted that: 'In addition to the seven children who are the subject of this serious case review, a further ten children, who had not been looked after, disclosed sexual abuse.'

Although in the majority of cases a single male perpetrator was involved, one review related to children living with two male foster carers, both of whom were subsequently convicted of sexual offences against the children in their care. In yet another, a child had been sexually abused by two separate sets of foster carers.

Children with serious health issues or a disability prior to serious harm or fatality

It has been widely acknowledged that children with disabilities are at greater risk of abuse and neglect than non-disabled children (Frederick *et al*, 2019; Sullivan and Knutson, 2000). This is due to a range of factors, including less knowledge or awareness of inappropriate behaviour; impairments in their ability to communicate what is happening to them;

greater mobility problems that limit their capacity to avoid an abuser; and the need for more personal care (Taylor *et al*, 2016).

In the present study, the reviews identified 23 of the 98 children (23%) as having a disability or serious health concern prior to the incident. In some cases, an individual child had more than one issue, for example, one little girl who was blind was also severely brain damaged. The proportion of children in this study who had serious health issues or a disability was higher than noted for fostered children generally. National statistics for 2018–19 showed that nine per cent of children living in foster care are disabled (Ofsted, 2020). The figures are small and the two samples not fully comparable, and it would be unwise to draw any conclusions.

Table 12: Type of disability or serious health issue prior to serious harm or fatality as recorded in the serious case reviews

Number of children n=23	Type of disability
11	Statement of SEN/physical and learning disability
5	ADHD and Asperger's/autism
2	Opiate addicted
2	Brain defect, damaged kidney
1	Birth injuries, deaf
1	Complex developmental trauma
1	Blind with severe brain damage

Table 12 shows that disabilities that affect learning and behaviour were most commonly recorded. Sixteen (70%) of the 23 children had a form of learning disability or experienced a combination of ADHD, Asperger's or autism. The gender of the child was known for 18 of the 23 children and showed twice as many boys (n=12) as girls (n=6). This is in line with commonly held opinion that the ratio of males to females with learning disabilities is approximately three to one. However, surveys using research data would suggest equal numbers of boys and girls, with the apparent differences being related to associated school behaviour problems (Adullah, 2018).

An examination of what happened to this group of children shows that eight children had died: four from physical injuries, two from severe neglect, one from poisoning, and one had committed suicide. A comparison with children without disabilities in the current sample suggests that these children may be more vulnerable. Thirty-five per cent of children with disabilities or serious health issues had died, compared with 15 per cent (11 of 75) of children without recorded disabilities.

Of the children with disabilities or serious health issues who had been maltreated, nine had suffered physical harm, five had been sexually abused and two had been severely neglected.

SUMMARY OF KEY FINDINGS

- There were 52 serious case reviews that met the criteria for inclusion in the current study: in 39 (75%) cases, children were living with foster carers, in seven (13%) with adopters, and in six (12%) with special guardians.

- In 46 of the 52 cases, children's social care had been involved at the time of the incident. Where there was no current involvement, children had been adopted, lived with special guardians, were on residence orders, or in a private fostering arrangement.

- A comparison of the findings from the present study with the wider sample included in the triennial analysis of serious case reviews (Brandon *et al*, 2020) shows some interesting differences. In the present study:

  - A higher proportion of reviews related to more than one child, a bias that reflects the number of historical cases in the sample.

  - A lower proportion of reviews related to child deaths – just over one-third (37%) of children had died during the period studied, compared with 62 per cent of the sample over a similar timeframe included in the triennial analysis.

  - Some two-thirds (64%) of children were over the age of five years, whereas practically the same proportion (63%) included in the triennial analysis related to children under the age of five years.

- In 23 of the 52 serious case reviews (42%), the review had identified concerns with the assessment of carers. The assessment process relating to special guardians was particularly problematic; concerns with the assessment had been recorded in all the six cases. Overall, for a slightly greater proportion of carers who went on to sexually abuse children, the review had recorded concerns over the assessment process.

- The 52 reviews involved 98 children, of whom 19 had died and 79 had suffered serious harm. A focus on the individual children enabled a greater understanding of their circumstances and highlighted the complexity of some cases.

- Age was a factor in child fatalities, but not their gender. In general, younger children had died as a result of physical abuse, extreme neglect or sudden unexpected death (SUDI), whereas it was older children (those over the age of 11 years) who had, knowingly or otherwise, killed themselves.

- The majority (62%) of children who had suffered serious harm had been sexually abused. A scrutiny of this group finds that children in middle to late childhood, living in foster care, were most vulnerable, particularly girls. Boys and girls were equally subjected to physical abuse. Of particular concern was the sexual abuse of numerous children by a single male carer.

- Children with disabilities were found to be particularly vulnerable. This group was both overrepresented in the sample compared with those in foster care generally and a greater proportion had been killed than children without disabilities.

Chapter 3
Pitfalls in selecting carers

The recruitment, assessment and approval of carers are responsibilities shared by many professionals and agencies in fostering and adoption services. All carry an overriding responsibility for safeguarding and promoting the welfare of children in need of their services, in accordance with national legislation in all parts of the UK and with the UN Convention on the Rights of the Child.

Marjorie Morrison (2018) begins her CoramBAAF guide for fostering and adoption panels in Scotland by focusing on the key responsibilities of selecting safe and competent carers for vulnerable children:

> At the heart of the work of adoption and fostering panels is concern for children who are separated from their birth parents and who need others to care for them. Those who provide that care within their own homes and families through fostering and adoption need to be carefully assessed and prepared before being approved for the task. For those children who are unable to return to their own parents, planning security for their future must be of the highest calibre.
>
> (Morrison, 2018, p.3)

The suitability of carers looking after the children in this study was an important issue that emerged in many of the serious case reviews. Questions were raised about the scope and thoroughness of assessment and approval processes (and the subsequent support, oversight and review of carers once the children had been placed with them).

RIGOROUS ASSESSMENT WITH A SAFEGUARDING FOCUS

The reviews found evidence of concern with regard to the assessment of potential carers, some identified early in the contact with them and others arising later in the recruitment process.

One report, where two male foster carers subsequently had received custodial sentences for sexual offences against children placed with them, concluded that:

> Two main elements were lacking in the checking process...One was the application of a safeguarding focus where the needs of vulnerable children were paramount. The other was that the information which was

gathered was not properly analysed, making reference to the extensive knowledge which is available to social workers about what contributes to successful fostering.

There were cases where concerns and information had been recorded, but not subjected to robust challenge, scrutiny and analysis during the assessment. In one case where a young child had been sexually abused by her foster carer, the review concluded: 'that when these key features [robust challenge, scrutiny and analysis] are absent, the approval of foster carers is compromised'.

Recommendations from these reviews call for far more rigorous assessment of potential carers, which should include a safeguarding perspective and a greater degree of scrutiny and analysis of information gathered.

ASSESSMENT IS 'AN ACTIVITY AND A PROCESS OF UNDERSTANDING'

From recruitment through to approval, the selection process is an interactive one between potential carers and professional staff. Assessment is described by Peter Reder and colleagues (1993) as 'both an activity in itself and a process of understanding' (p.83). It allows professional staff to begin to get to know and understand the applicants, in order to form a judgement about their suitability as carers. It also allows applicants to withdraw at any stage as they become more familiar with what is expected of them and the challenges they may face.

The reviews found that some potential carers had formed a negative view of the recruitment and approval processes and had found them difficult and intrusive. Absences or changes of key staff, at practitioner or management level, or other organisational pressures had caused anxiety or uncertainty for applicants and a loss of trust.

The assessment took approximately eight months to complete, two months more than the recommended six months, but there were extenuating circumstances due to the assessor's brief period of sick leave, and her undertaking other additional duties.

Adoption UK's Adoption Barometer, following a survey of 3,500 adopters across the UK, reported that '50 per cent of prospective adopters found the [approvals and matching] process as a whole so difficult that they wondered if they could continue' (Adoption UK, 2019, p.7). In the same survey, 58 per cent of prospective adopters reported delays in their approval process, 'most of which were caused by administrative difficulties or other factors within their adoption agencies' (Adoption UK, 2019, p.7). Mary Baginsky and colleagues (2017) found similar complaints from studies of foster care applicants, who reported delays and excessive paperwork, as well as giving feedback on the intrusive nature of the process.

The assessment process provides opportunities for professional staff working with potential carers to identify those who would not be suitable and to help them understand why. The most recent findings (Ofsted, 2020) show that 39 per cent of completed applications to become foster carers were approved in the year 2018–19, which included applications to both local authority and independent fostering services. Sixty per cent were withdrawn: two-thirds by the applicant and one-third by the agency, and one per cent were rejected by the agency (Ofsted, 2020, Figure 5; terminology as quoted by Ofsted).

As part of the process, sensitive issues about family history, experience and relationships need to be fully explored with the applicants. Adoption guidance in England, for example, recognises that 'matters the prospective adopter might consider unimportant may be of greater significance than they realise' (Statutory Guidance on Adoption, 3.22, DfE, 2013a). Mary Baginsky and colleagues reinforce this point: 'While some intrusion is inevitable, it is important to explain to applicants why it is necessary' (Baginsky *et al*, 2017, p.8).

However, the reviews showed that there was a further very small group of potential carers who appeared committed and co-operative with the staff of the fostering or adoption services, but who chose not to share all their history or to be entirely open about themselves and personal family difficulties (discussed in Chapter 6, *Smoke and mirrors*).

In one review, the withholding of critical information by a potential foster carer during her assessment illustrates how approval of carers can be compromised. Her inability to be honest and transparent at this stage was considered by the review to have continued to reverberate once she and her husband had been approved as foster carers. This had tragic consequences. Nearly four years later, the foster mother pleaded guilty to the manslaughter of a two-year-old child who had been placed with her and her husband three months previously. No contra-indications had emerged in the original approval of these foster carers. However, the review recorded:

> ...it is significant to note that the fostering assessment did not include that the foster mother had experienced postnatal depression and... had attempted suicide following the breakdown of her [previous] marriage. Whilst it is not uncommon for prospective foster carers to have experienced significant emotional difficulties in their past, it is expected that these issues are raised by the prospective carers and fully explored with the fostering social worker in order to determine whether the issues had been resolved, and the carers would be able to manage

the challenges of fostering. In this case such disclosure of relevant past information did not happen.

An Independent Inquiry in another case (included in this study) considered the very complex issues following the custodial sentences of two male foster carers for sexual activity involving children who had been placed with them.

We are not saying that the Council would have found out at that early stage that CF and IW were potential paedophiles if the Council had applied a safeguarding focus...Instead, we suggest that more systematic and rigorous checking might have unearthed more information, which might have created some "alert" in the system, which could have been recorded and referred to later when concrete concerns began to emerge...An approach which was informed more strongly by the safeguarding of children would have given CF and IW a message about the "tightness" of the fostering services' systems and layers of oversight and scrutiny to which they would be subject.

Following some high profile reviews of child maltreatment in the last two decades, concepts such as "need for vigilance", "keeping an open mind" and "respectful uncertainty" have become an important part of the language of safeguarding practice. A consistent message from the reviews in this study is the importance of rigorous gathering and cross-checking of information about potential carers, and meticulous recording, analysis and reflection.

The need to strengthen recruitment processes and procedures and to make them safer is a conclusion reached by Nina Biehal and colleagues (2014) in their study for the NSPCC of allegations of abuse made against foster carers and residential workers.

In a small number of very serious cases involving the persistent neglect, emotional and/or sexual abuse of children, it was clear that the foster carers concerned should never have been recruited. High quality assessment, recruitment and review procedures are needed to prevent these individuals being able to harm children.

(Biehal *et al*, 2014, p.13)

However, there is and always will be an element of risk involved in selecting carers; dedicated, experienced professionals will be deceived by applicants who have withheld information and not been transparent or honest with them. This can happen even when all the processes leading to a decision to approve potential carers have been carried out thoroughly and to a high standard. As Malcolm Gladwell concludes from his work on making sense of strangers, 'We need to accept that the search to understand a stranger has real limits. We will never know the whole truth. We might have to be satisfied with something short of that' (Gladwell, 2019, p.261).

This is the conundrum with which professionals and their organisations have to live.

CHALLENGING AREAS FOR EXPLORATION IN RECRUITMENT

In recruiting and assessing potential carers to look after vulnerable children, it is essential that practitioners gain an understanding of their motivation, confront any contradictory or conflicting information, and fully explore sensitive issues.

Motivation for caring for other people's children

It is well understood that the reasons prompting adults to offer to care for a child or children who are not their own, within their own homes and families, are likely to be complex and diverse. Marjorie Morrison gives a flavour of this complexity in relation to foster care:

> Some applicants may be responding to a mix of enjoying the experience of caring along with the knowledge that the fees offered and the training given provide a career path. Others may have very personal motives rooted in their own life experiences. This may include personal views on areas such as helping to keep siblings together or providing opportunities for a child with a disability. Offers of kinship care often emerge from some very complex family agendas.

(Morrison, 2018, p.70)

Guidance emphasises that motivation needs to be explored thoroughly with applicants, and then carefully considered and analysed (CoramBAAF, 2019). Income, employment status, following on a family tradition, the desire to create a family, wanting to help vulnerable children, being part of a professional community – these can all be very different motivating factors and there may well be a combination of several.

In a few cases in this study, the link between the need for income and prospective foster carers' motivation and choices was apparent early in their assessment.

> Perpetrator 1 and his wife were approved by [the] Family Placement Scheme as Project Carers. This scheme paid carers an enhanced rate for providing intensive care and support to young people who were deemed to have the most challenging behaviour and needed highly skilled foster care support. This is significant as a theme throughout the fostering file is the view that Perpetrator 1 and his wife were willing to work with young people that other carers had given up on...The family were in some financial difficulties...

Motivation for applicants to adopt may be no less complex, but is different from that of potential foster carers, and requires equally careful exploration and analysis.

> *In adoption, the clear purpose is for the child to become a full member of a new family and the fundamental motive of applicants usually centres on forming their family. The assessment task is firstly, to ensure that their understanding of the pathway chosen to do this stands up to the reality; and secondly, to ensure that, where applicants are a couple, both partners are equally motivated.*

(Morrison, 2018, p.70)

Sometimes it is not clear whether applicants are more interested in adoption or fostering. Such issues should be carefully explored right from the beginning with a 'full examination of motivation'.

With the changes in legislation and regulations, there are now various routes to securing permanence for a child, including concurrent planning, "twin track" or "parallel" planning, and Fostering for Adoption, which may result in the child being fostered, adopted or cared for under a child arrangements order or special guardianship order (some of these are applicable only in England).

An example reinforcing the importance of exploring motivation is found in the Independent Inquiry into Child Sexual Abuse (2019). It cites a case (also included in the present study) involving sexual abuse by a male carer working in residential and foster care between 1982 and 1990.

> *Campbell's approval did not follow the established process, legitimate concerns about his motivation were ignored and he was not subject to re-approval as he should have been. His abuse of children might have been prevented had processes been followed.*

(Independent Inquiry into Child Sexual Abuse, 2019, p.139)

The importance of consulting the children of potential carers was stressed in one serious case review. Assessing children's wishes and feelings and any particular needs, and considering the consequences for them should a child be placed with their family, was shown to be highly relevant in securing the well-being of all family members, including their safety and security. In this case, the adopters had three boys of their own when a little girl of five years was placed with them. The "middle" boy had cerebral palsy. He was subsequently convicted of inflicting multiple stab wounds on the girl. The review concluded:

> *In the adoption assessment process, all existing children of prospective adoptive parents should be fully assessed...All members of the adoptive family should be consulted individually on the impact of the placement before an adoption application is made.*

Perhaps of particular significance in relation to this study and the complex motivation of prospective carers are the circumstances of children who were harmed by their special guardians. These issues are addressed in the final section of this chapter.

Gaps in information

In several cases, the reviews found that the process of assessment had not been adequately undertaken. There had been too much reliance placed on what the applicants had told the assessing social workers, with not enough cross-referencing of this information with other sources of evidence, such as family members or friends, local authority or criminal records, or by asking questions of referees. In some cases, referees had not been seen, references had been accepted at face value, and family members not interviewed.

> *The information covered a wide variety of areas pertaining to Mr and Mrs George, with the vast majority of information taken directly from the words of the couple...there were other areas of the couple's life that should have posed questions in relation to their honesty...None of these issues were raised by managers, panel members, or by the agency decision-makers. Consequently, there was no interrogation of these secrets and dishonesties, and no analysis of the possible implications.*

In another case, where a male foster carer was subsequently arrested for sexual and physical assault of young people in his and his wife's care over a number of years, it was found that the original assessment was:

> *...primarily based upon the information supplied by Mr and Mrs F. There was no verification of information presented with the referees. It is clear that there were issues from their family history that needed further exploration, but there was no analysis in relation to the likely impact of these experiences on their functioning as adults, parents and their ability to re-parent a child.*

Referees' comments may suggest a gap in information given by the applicants or that further issues need to be discussed. In the following case, the foster mother pleaded guilty to the manslaughter of the two-year-old child who had been placed with her and her husband three months earlier. The reviewers found that:

> *The assessment of the foster carers met key requirements of the Fostering Regulations 2002. The references raised no issues. The only negative comment at this point was from a family friend who felt the foster father might not be as committed to fostering as the foster mother, and that they had not been together as a couple for very long.*

This reinforces the importance of cross-checking and triangulating sources of evidence.

Behaviour, attitudes and professional responses

In a number of cases, there was an early indication of issues of concern and professional unease about one or both foster carer applicants. This was often as the result of their hostility or more subtle, inappropriate behaviour or resistance, such as refusing to attend preparatory training programmes or to engage with other requirements.

Such behaviours were very often, but not always, exhibited by the male applicant. It would seem from accounts in the reviews that assessment interviews were normally held with both applicants together rather than separately. This would suggest the importance of interviewing applicants individually as well as together. One review noted:

> [An issue] in relation to work with foster carers is the danger of considering them as "the foster carers" rather than individuals in their own right. From the start of the assessment it is important to consider each as an individual...the pattern seems to have been established of viewing them as a unit.

In another case, a male foster carer and his wife had been registered foster carers since the early 1970s, with a gap of a few years in the mid-1980s due to marital difficulties, and they applied to be re-approved. The records in the local authority were found by the serious case review to hold significant information about an earlier assault charge, racist comments and reluctance to engage with a new review system. None of this had been explored as part of their subsequent assessment and approval as foster carers.

> The recruitment process picked up on Perpetrator 1's controlling behaviour but failed to address it, thus allowing him early on to gain an inappropriate level of power within the system. There seems to have been an approach which was one of giving the carers the "benefit of the doubt" and engaging with them as colleagues.

The male carer was found to have been a serial sex offender and was convicted of 18 offences of historical sexual abuse and received a custodial sentence.

Other examples suggest that fundamental issues of power and authority can arise in relationships between social work staff and the potential carers, even at an early stage in the assessment. If left unrecognised, unchallenged and unmanaged, they could have damaging or tragic consequences for the child or children placed with the carers.

> During the fostering assessment and approval, initial concerns about the male applicant's belligerent attitude and self-confessed difficulty in dealing with authority figures were not properly explored.

The importance at an early stage of addressing issues of power and authority and inappropriate behaviour, either demonstrated in the relationship and interaction between the potential carers or with fostering and adoption professional staff, are considered by some of the reviews. One review noted "authoritative practice" as a theme threaded throughout its findings.

> How far professionals were able to work authoritatively with Mr and Mrs F and therefore act to ensure the best interests of children in their care were being met? The authoritative worker is one who is clear about required standards, assumes appropriate control yet is also empathetic and responsive to the needs of the family.

These issues are seen as fundamental to the skills and expertise required generally by social workers and recently reinforced in the Professional Standards Guidance issued by Social Work England.

> Social workers need to be able to recognise and respond to behaviour that may indicate resistance to change, and a lack of co-operation, and take action where necessary, particularly where this is linked to safeguarding concerns.

(Social Work England, 2019)

Contradictory accounts from applicants

It was not unusual for the reviews to find contradictions in accounts given by potential carers about their experiences as children or adults or their family history, for factual information to be glossed over or for issues to be downplayed. Careful listening and recording, and time for reflection and the use of supervision, can lead to such contradictions being identified, challenged and explored, and the implications for the applicants' capacity to parent vulnerable children being better understood.

The review concerning Claire, a young child sexually abused by her foster father, found 'clear issues' regarding both potential carers' unresolved relationships with their own parents, which 'were not commented on or explored during their assessment':

> ...the couple described [their] childhoods in very positive terms... However, from both carers' accounts, there were indications that these childhoods were not quite as they were described...There was information contained within the assessment of the foster carers that was presented to panel which suggested this was a family where secrets and dishonesties were an accepted part of life.

In another review, a male foster carer had been found guilty of offences of rape and indecent assault of a foster child and a family member. Reviewing the assessment of this carer and his wife, which had taken place some years earlier, a number of concerning issues were revealed, presenting a very different picture from that which had been told to the assessors. These had not been explored at the time. They included the wife's unhappy childhood and some marital discord, as well as her resentment of health visitors and other health professionals. Two references had been taken up, both of which were negative.

> One reference wondered how they [the potential carers] would cope with fostering as they were not very organised and would not seek help if needed, and the other thought that Perpetrator 2 was a "Peter Pan" figure who preferred the company of young people and his wife was unsure of herself. Instead of exploring these issues further, two more references were sought which provided positive comments.

Sensitive areas

A number of the serious case reviews highlighted the complexity and sensitivity of effective assessment in relation to potential carers where issues of ethnicity, culture, language, religion, gender, sexual orientation, single parenting, physical and/or mental health, and disability needed to be explored. Several of these factors may feature together in the households of potential carers and, in this study, this was often the case, as noted by one review:

> Aspects of race, culture and religion are complex in this case: and in addition both [foster carers] were disabled people.

This review identified three key issues:

- *the lack of comprehensive assessment of these factors when the applicants were first assessed as foster carers;*

- *the tendency for a one dimensional approach, mainly focused on religion, that ignored the whole life experience of the person concerned;*

- *the powerful impact that fear of being accused of discrimination in relation to race and disability can have on judgements and interventions.*

Discomfort or reluctance among inexperienced professionals to probe for further information and evidence was also apparent in other reviews. In one case, there were a number of sensitive issues that needed to be addressed with the applicants. Two men had applied to become foster carers, having lived together in a relationship for seven years. They owned their own house, and wanted children and a family of their own. The older of the two had suffered an industrial accident six years previously and had not worked since then. His disability limited his activities and mobility, and he was also a heavy smoker. Their family histories suggested complex childhood experiences for both of them.

The reviewers, in this case, outlined the following issues that would be helpful to explore when assessing same-sex couples.

- *Full examination of motivation and in particular issues around whether their underlying aim was to be parents (adoption) or temporary carers (fostering).*

- *Exploration of childhood experiences, experiences of being parented, the nature of applicants' attachments to their primary caregivers and the way in which these have influenced adult relationships.*

- *Exploration of sibling relationships through childhood and adulthood.*

- *Gender, sex and sexuality.*

- *The individual's experience of homosexuality, their own response to this and the response of their family, all need to be open and fully discussed.*

- *How confident they feel in relation to their sexual orientation, how comfortable they are as gay men or women, and how they constructively manage homophobia in their own lives.*

- *How they would help a child who experienced prejudice because of their carers' sexual orientation.*

- *Partnerships and relationships, which should include sexual relationships and previous significant partnerships.*

- *How they would support a child with their own emerging sexuality in adolescence and ensure an appropriate sex education.*

The way in which sensitive issues are introduced and potential carers are supported in addressing them with assessors is critical. To do so effectively, skilled professional staff need expert supervision and to be given time for analysis and reflection. A lack of time and heavy workloads have been identified as barriers to effective supervision (Rothwell *et al*, 2019). Organisations need to recognise the importance of the knowledge, training and skills of professional staff, as well as the provision of appropriate resources to achieve this. CoramBAAF has produced useful resources for social workers, managers and all those involved in the recruitment, assessment and support of lesbian and gay carers and adopters (see BAAF/New Family Social, 2013 and de Jong and Donnelly, 2015).

INFORMATION REQUIRES CRITICAL APPRAISAL AND ANALYSIS

As discussed in the Introduction, the serious case reviews in this study were published between 2007 and 2019 but, in many cases, refer to events spanning several years before and involving carers who were approved two or three decades earlier. Many reviews stressed the importance of professional staff rigorously following assessment and approval processes, but some reviews also questioned the effectiveness of the processes themselves and whether they were still fit for purpose or needed review and improvement, based on new knowledge, practical experience and research evidence.

Assessment infrastructure – use of Form F

The Prospective Foster Carer Report (Form F) was designed for the assessment of prospective foster carers in England (similar forms exist for Scotland, Wales and Northern Ireland). Form F was last updated in 2018 and the accompanying guidance notes in 2019 (CoramBAAF, 2019).

The study found that one serious case review, published in 2017, made particular comment about the way in which information about potential carers was structured and the lack of emphasis on analysing the information collected. This review concluded:

> *The assessment and approval of foster carers is a critical cornerstone in how children are safeguarded and how their needs are met. Many foster carers are successfully recruited across the country and provide a high standard of care to vulnerable children. The assessment form in use lists the foster care standards and competencies required by national guidance, and this is appropriate. However, the lack of emphasis on critical appraisal and analysis of this information creates potential loopholes that undermine the quality of decision-making when the question of suitability is decided.*

The review asserted that:

> *...despite the calls to improve the quality of fostering assessments and recommendations to move to a "value-based" or "adult attachment style" of assessment (NSPCC, 2013), there is no research and no local or national data on this issue.*

In 2018, the older version of Form F was replaced by a new edition (CoramBAAF, 2019). Additionally, the guide designed to help assessors in England to complete a comprehensive and evidence-based assessment, using Form F, was updated (Chapman, 2019). Similar guides are available for Wales and Scotland.

Formats for recording references, analysis and action

References are seen as another important building block in creating a comprehensive picture of potential carers, and finding out about their strengths, commitment and relationships, and how they respond to problems and resolve difficulties. The value of references, however, depends on from whom they are obtained and how they are recorded, analysed and used to inform the assessment and approval process. In some of the serious case reviews, concerns were expressed about the absence of structured formats for written statements and visits to referees, although this has now changed (CoramBAAF, 2019). Referees in one case in 2007 had been a neighbour and friend of the applicants, and no present or past employers had been approached.

> *Neither referee was asked to make any written comment upon the dynamics and stability of the applicants' relationship and whether they had any information to suggest that either CF or IW could pose a risk to children.*

EFFECTIVENESS OF FOSTERING AND ADOPTION PANELS

Concerns were expressed in some reviews about the effectiveness of fostering and adoption panels in the particular circumstances of the case they were reviewing. The current systems in place provide opportunities for comprehensive information collection, cross-checking and analysis, with several layers of quality assurance for scrutiny and challenge from the assessing social worker, through the multi-disciplinary fostering or adoption panel to the agency decision-maker (DfE, 2013b).

More than one review commented on the performance of panels and identified insufficient detailed scrutiny and challenge as a key theme.

> *The fostering panel could usefully have adopted a far more challenging and questioning approach to the assessments of both foster carers, specifically in relation to the level of reliance on self-reported information, the particular issues related to diversity, and the fact that both applicants would be learning skills for the first time as untested carers...*

> *For this system to work safely, in approving suitable foster carers and protecting children from harm, the vital role played by scrutiny and challenge must be fully realised and consistently delivered.*

Knowledgeable and expert practice guidance for developing effective fostering and adoption panels is available from CoramBAAF (Lord and Cullen, 2016; Morrison, 2018; Borthwick and Lord, 2019). Although some aspects of the fostering and adoption regulations and guidance may be nation-specific, agencies throughout the UK will find many of the practice points highly relevant, informative and applicable.

MANAGING DIFFERENCES OF OPINION

Contradictions can occur during the assessment process in the views and judgements of the professionals involved. In the serious case reviews, there were some instances of differences of opinion: between staff in a local authority and an independent fostering provider undertaking recruitment and assessment of carers; between two health professionals located in different agencies; and between children's social care professionals with different roles and perspectives working in the same agency. These suggest the importance of acknowledging and recording differences that occur, examining the evidence, and bringing these issues into open discussion with managers or with the fostering or adoption panels. Ignoring such differences and not taking any action to explore or resolve them can have negative consequences.

For example, one review recorded how, in the early 1990s, the doubts held by a General Practitioner about the suitability of a potential foster carer had been ignored or overruled during the assessment:

> *A GP expressed misgivings to a social worker about Mrs F's ability to cope with another child because of a health condition and the severity of her son's problems. Following further discussions between the GP and the medical adviser to the fostering panel, the medical adviser had concluded that Mr and Mrs F were fit to foster and they were recommended for approval to the panel.*

Sixteen years later, following a number of allegations of physical and sexual abuse, some of which were withdrawn, Mr F was found guilty of the sexual abuse of one child and the physical assault of four others in his care.

ASSESSMENT OF CARERS IN CHANGING CIRCUMSTANCES

One of the notable findings of this study was the number of instances in which foster carers, who had already been approved, were required to undergo a further assessment. Adopters when seeking to adopt another child are similarly required to undergo a further assessment.

Reference has already been made to cases of foster carers who, for various reasons, had ceased fostering and then sought re-approval, sometimes years later. Foster carers also transferred to other local authority fostering services or to independent fostering providers.

There were multiple instances of carers seeking to change the legal status of a child or children living with them, for example, applying for a residence order (now a child arrangements order), seeking to adopt a child or children, or applying for a special guardianship order. Such applications required the carers to be assessed again. It can be argued that the applications were motivated by the desire of carers to provide greater stability and permanence for the children.

The reviews of these cases identified that "experienced carers" might not be given the same level of scrutiny in a further assessment. Similarly, the impact that a change of legal status, if granted, would have on the local authority's responsibility for the child was not always fully considered. As with fostering reviews, a further assessment can provide an important opportunity to step back and consider the motivation of the carers, their strengths and capacities in the context of current care responsibilities and the consequences for the child or children concerned. Is the proposed change in these children's best interests? A return to the case of Mr and Mrs F provides an example:

The decision [of the local authority] to support Mr and Mrs F's application for residence orders is with hindsight very surprising. It would have assisted social workers in their assessment if they had been aware of the mental health issues that were known to the GP. Consideration should have been given to the impact on their capacity to foster. The failure to act upon the alleged domestic abuse also prevented a full assessment of the children's situation; had this been known it may have influenced the decision by children's social care to support Mr and Mrs F's application for residence orders.

Another case involved a long-term, single foster carer with an adopted teenage son, who had applied for residence orders for two of the children living with her. One of the children was a six-year-old girl who, unknown to the authorities, had been sexually abused by the adopted son for two years prior to the application for the residence order being made. The abuse continued for a further two years after the residence order had been granted. The local authority had agreed the application. The Independent Overview Report commented:

...that although the legal arrangements are very different, the practical impact of making residence orders was similar to making an adoption order. However, the thorough investigations, assessment and decision-making processes that would be required before an adoption order is made did not take place. No details of the carer's emotional, physical and mental health were available to the court and nor were adequate details of the standards in the foster home or the conduct and behaviour of the perpetrator who was living in the household.

The review recommended that, in the circumstances of an application for a residence order which, if granted, 'would discharge a care order', the local authority should introduce a number of measures and 'as a minimum, a careful and thorough formal assessment'.

A further assessment must also take place when carers move from their current local authority fostering to an independent fostering provider or another local authority. In the case of Mr and Mrs F, quoted above, after the residence orders had been granted, they left their local authority fostering service to work with an independent fostering provider and underwent a further assessment.

The Form F was completed by an independent social worker who noted that Mr and Mrs F were experienced foster carers...The outcome of the assessment was positive and there is no mention of any medical problems.

It is not uncommon for foster carers to transfer from one local authority to another. Such a move 'usually requires foster carers to repeat fully the same approval and assessment process' (Lawson and Cann, 2019, p.27). The reviews of a number of cases found the further assessment cursory or incomplete.

A UK-wide survey by the Fostering Network (Lawson and Cann, 2019), found that 92 per cent of carers who transferred to different services in the last three years found it a time-consuming process. They had to once again go through the whole approval process, taking on average six months to complete. Thorough assessment of carers, who are transferring to another service and are already well known to local health and children's social care services, can be seen as an unnecessary additional burden to stretched and pressured services: 'I am redoing the assessment but it has taken eight months just to get references!' It also takes its toll on foster carers who said that they had to redo "everything":

> *References from family and friends, they met with them, interviewed them, they looked at our bank accounts, they asked intimate questions about our marriage and family relationships, they went through the whole invasive process again, from scratch.*

> (Lawson and Cann, 2019, p.27)

The Fostering Network concluded that the responses they received in the survey demonstrate why reform of the assessment process when foster carers move to different services is badly needed (Lawson and Cann, 2019).

Such further assessment of carers, whether they transfer to other fostering services or seek to change the legal status of children placed with them, brings some sharply divided perspectives. The view of some experienced carers is that a lighter touch or perhaps a modified assessment can be used. The Fostering Network sees the need to reform the process. However, many of the serious case reviews in this study called for rigour and thoroughness in light of what was happening or went on to happen to already vulnerable children. This is obviously an issue for further examination and debate.

SELECTION OF SPECIAL GUARDIANS

The assessment of special guardians differs significantly from that relating to foster carers or adopters. Special guardians are assessed for their suitability to look after a particular child. As such, the assessment must explore the potential special guardian's knowledge, experience and expectations of the child as well as their relationship with the child.

Six serious case reviews in this study concerned 10 children who had suffered maltreatment while living with people appointed as their special guardians. Two of the children had died. The reviews were completed between 2016 and 2019. There were concerns about the selection of special guardians in all six reviews.

Special guardianship orders (SGOs) are a relatively recent addition to the alternative care arrangements available for children living in England and Wales who are unable to remain with their birth parents. They were introduced in the Adoption and Children Act 2002 and implemented in 2005, primarily:

> ...as a private law route to legal permanence for children unable to live with their birth parents...They were intended to complement adoption and originally envisaged as a legal option for older children who had existing relationships with family or where adoption was unsuitable for religious or cultural reasons.

(Harwin *et al*, 2015, p.2)

Harwin and colleagues reported that during the period 2010 to 2017, 'a total of 21,504 children found homes with relatives or family friends on an SGO as a result of s.31 care proceedings,' and added: 'it is quite clear that SGOs now occupy a major place in the menu of permanency orders' (Harwin *et al*, 2019, p.41). If the child has been in the care of a local authority, once the order is made, the child ceases to be looked after by that local authority.

Concerns that the use of special guardianship was not developing as originally intended led the DfE to launch a review in 2015, on the grounds that:

> ...special guardianship was being used for very young children and usurping the role of adoption, that children were being placed with people with whom they had no strong ties and that assessments were rushed and did not consider the child's long-term needs (Department for Education, 2015).

(Harwin *et al*, 2019, p.19)

Professionals, consulted as part of the DfE review, gave a consistent message when comparing the assessment processes and support for special guardians with those for adopters:

> Whereas adopters receive preparation, a lengthier assessment, and information on the child including a health assessment, there is no such requirement for special guardianship.

(Harwin *et al*, 2019, p.15)

Brandon and colleagues, in their triennial analysis of serious case reviews, expressed similar concerns:

> *If necessary, the proceedings should be extended and there should be a trial placement. This is especially the case if the child has not previously lived with the proposed carers.*

(Brandon *et al*, 2020, p.19)

Professionals were very concerned about the lack of rigour in assessments of prospective special guardians and, in particular, considered that the 26-week statutory timeframe for completion (in England and Wales) resulted in rushed assessments and, in some cases, premature decisions about the suitability of special guardians.

Assessing potential special guardians

Each of the six serious case reviews relating to children who had died or had been seriously harmed while living with special guardians identified particular issues that impacted negatively on the assessment process. The barriers to a full understanding of the strengths and weaknesses of potential carers applied to both family and friends and those who were not related to the child.

Keeping the child within the family

The reviews found that, when the potential special guardian was related to the child, decisions about their approval may have been driven by the presumption that it was in the child's best interests to be cared for within their birth family. There were two cases where the review clearly identified that this disproportionately influenced the assessment decisions. The case of Bonnie serves as an illustration.

CASE STUDY: BONNIE

Bonnie was living with her maternal grandmother, who had been appointed as her special guardian.

Bonnie's mother had a learning disability, lived a chaotic lifestyle and 'had limited ability to recognise the needs of her children'. When Bonnie was born, she was subject to a child protection plan and at the age of three months, she was placed in the care of her maternal grandmother under a voluntary care agreement. Following care proceedings, the local authority sought a special guardianship order, naming Bonnie's maternal grandmother as the potential special guardian.

The assessment was not easy; the family history and circumstances were complex and there were discussions between colleagues on the family's comparative risk and resilience factors. This included Bonnie's grandfather, who had a series of unproven allegations of sexual abuse made against him. However, he had not lived in the home for 12 years and the grandmother 'had full understanding that the grandfather should have no contact'. One practitioner recalled, 'This was not a simple assessment, there were many complex components'.

The grandmother was fully co-operative and seen as compliant and trustworthy, so the conclusion of the professionals involved was 'that there was just enough evidence to "tip the balance" in favour of the grandmother taking care of Bonnie'. The special guardianship order had stringent requirements for support and monitoring.

Although having assured children's social care that she would not allow her husband to return to the household, the grandmother accepted Bonnie's grandfather back to live with them. Bonnie was two years old when found to have been sexually abused by him. The review concluded:

It is apparent that the CAFCASS Independent Guardian and Social Worker A, and perhaps the court, worked to the presumption that a child's best interest is generally to be cared for within their natural family, with the assessment appearing to seek evidence supporting permanency with grandmother rather than making any comparison with alternative options.

Over-reliance on information supplied by potential special guardians

The reviews highlighted that an over-reliance on the information given by potential special guardians can result in poorly informed assessments. Information should be gathered from a variety of sources, supplemented and cross-checked.

Three of the reviews of children living with special guardians identified these issues. The case of Child LH provides an example of the negative consequences that can arise from relying solely on information from a single source.

CASE STUDY: CHILD LH

Four-year-old LH had lived with a special guardian (his aunt) for 18 months before his abuse became known.

As with many children subject to harm in this study, LH's family circumstances were complex, and there was more than one local authority involved. LH, when living with his mother, had been on a child protection plan under the category of neglect. An interim supervision order was granted nine months later, with the plan to place the child under a special guardianship order.

The review identified a number of critical issues about the special guardian order assessment process. The initial viability assessment of the maternal aunt (Ms X), undertaken by LH's home authority, had been positive, but there was worrying information that had not been explored.

There were professional concerns and doubts as the full assessment progressed, countered by the aunt, who gave plausible explanations, and checks had not been completed at the time of the court presentation. In addition, LH's mother, who had learning needs, did not want her sister to have the care of her young child.

The full SGO assessment of Ms X was underway in November 2015 and at this time Children Social Care received a letter from Child LH's mother re Ms X. The letter complained about Ms X as a carer and explicitly refused consent for her to be the carer for any of her children.

LH's aunt was charged with his assault (43 injuries found consistent with non-accidental injuries), pleaded guilty and received a 20-month custodial sentence, suspended for 18 months. The review highlighted a number of questions about the assessment in its analysis of practice:

- The robustness of the quality assurance measures in place to enable the successful assessment and approval of special guardianship carers.

- The importance of checks to supplement the information for special guardianship order assessments.

- The threshold for including non-conviction related information on a Disclosure and Barring Service (DBS) check.

- Advocacy for parents with a learning disability.

Assessment of non-related carers of children looked after

Special guardianship orders may also be granted to foster carers or other non-related carers for a child whom they are already looking after. The following case suggests that the assessment of carers well known to professionals may be subject to less scrutiny than would be otherwise expected.

> **CASE STUDY: P FAMILY**
>
> Four siblings had been removed from their mother in a neighbouring authority, due to physical and sexual abuse, and placed with foster carers who were employed by an independent fostering provider.
>
> Two years later, the children were made the subject of a final care order. Four years after that, the carers were successful in seeking special guardianship orders on all four children, having been 'assessed very positively' by the neighbouring authority: 'They were described as "exemplary" carers.' Three years on, all four siblings were removed due to concerns about the carers' parenting capacity, their mental health, domestic abuse, and the children's allegations and retractions of physical abuse.
>
> *The judge in this case commented that a serious case review should be considered, in light of long-standing concerns regarding the foster carers with an independent fostering agency, breakdown of placements involving other children placed with them in 2004, 2005 and allegations of abuse to one child from 2004–2008. Concerns also included assessment of the carers as special guardians by the neighbouring authority.*

An emerging theme identified by the review was the impact of the special guardians' behaviours 'in the way they were able to influence decision making. There was evidence of disguised compliance (Reder *et al*, 2009), manipulation and coercion of both professionals and the children in their care by both SG parents.' This has been a recurring theme in many of the reviews included in this study, as is further discussed in Chapter 6, *Smoke and Mirrors*.

KEY ISSUES RELATING TO THE ASSESSMENT OF POTENTIAL SPECIAL GUARDIANS

A number of critical issues stand out from examining these six reviews. It is clear that the families in the reviews had complicated histories and lived in complex circumstances. This was so whether the prospective special guardian was closely related to the child concerned, a distant relative, or their foster carer. In this respect, the family circumstances are generally no different to the families of other children in this study who were in foster care or adopted. However, the policy and practice context in which prospective special guardians were being selected is very different. As several of the reviews recorded, it appeared that placement with a relative or connected person was the preferred permanence option in any circumstances.

The prospective special guardians all demonstrated complex motivations for taking on the (often unplanned) care of a child and assuming the responsibilities of a special guardian. These motivations require careful understanding and exploration of the risks and challenges. This takes time, training, skill and experience, as has been seen with the selection and approval of foster carers and adopters. There also appears to be no good reason why private law special guardianship order applications made by a relative or foster carer require that the child should have lived with them for a minimum of 12 months, but the same does not apply to a child subject to care proceedings.

The reviews revealed that children's views about what was happening to them and the plans for their future living arrangements were often neither sought nor discussed with them, even when they were making themselves clear at a very young age. Similarly, when birth parent/s expressed views about prospective special guardians, these were apparently neither heard nor taken into account, nor the reasons for concerns fully explored. These issues are developed in the following chapters.

The children in these reviews were vulnerable children who had already experienced disruption in their care, and either abuse or neglect, and for whom the local authority had a child protection plan, or a supervision or care order. The local authority has a duty to act in these children's best interests. There is no good reason for the requirements in assessing prospective special guardians to be any less rigorous and thorough than those for selecting and approving foster carers and adopters, carried out by trained and experienced professionals, and supported by a process of checking and oversight at a senior level.

The issues about selecting special guardians have been considered in the review by the Nuffield Family Justice Observatory (Simmonds et al, 2019) and in the DfE triennial analysis of serious case reviews (Brandon et al, 2020). Priority recommendations were made by Simmonds and colleagues (2019) about the urgent action needed where a special guardianship order was being made as a conclusion to care proceedings. These included the following actions in relation to assessments:

- *Assessments should not be concluded until sufficient preparation has been completed.*

- *Developing the skills and knowledge of children's social workers in family placement must be prioritised.*

- *Ensure that viability assessments are appropriately robust and undertaken by a skilled professional.*

- *Ensure that the local authority agrees a plan with the prospective special guardian about the assessment process.*

- *Establish a robust protocol that ensures that the prospective special guardian has –or develops – a significant relationship with the child, including day-to-day care of the child, and that this forms the evidence base for making of the order.*

(Simmonds *et al*, 2019, p.18)

SUMMARY OF KEY FINDINGS

- Selecting safe, capable and nurturing carers for vulnerable children who are separated from their birth parents and needing others to care for them, is a fundamentally important responsibility of fostering and adoption services and for those appointing special guardians for a child. In 22 of the 52 serious case reviews, concerns about the quality of the assessments of potential carers were identified. The need for rigorous assessments that have a safeguarding focus was a strong theme emerging from the reviews.

- Assessment is an interactive process between the potential carers and professional staff. It is the act of gathering evidence and developing an understanding on which to judge the suitability of the potential carers to provide a child with a safe and caring environment.

- There will always be an element of risk involved in selecting carers. When applicants provide contradictory evidence or withhold significant information, they can mislead even experienced and dedicated professionals. Assessments may be inadequate when there is an overreliance on applicants' own reports. The information they provide must be cross-referenced with facts from other sources.

- If assessments are to be rigorous, they must explore a number of challenging areas. A key issue is the motivation of applicants to take on caring for other people's children. A range of factors will drive potential carers, both positive and negative, and must be fully explored during the assessment process.

- The behaviour of potential carers may trigger a sense of professional unease and uncertainty that should not be ignored. This may in some cases suggest a lack of commitment by one of the carers (if part of a couple), making it essential that applicants are seen separately as well as together. In other instances, the behaviour of potential carers may reflect a need to control their relationship with professionals. It is essential that professionals are able to work authoritatively with potential carers to ensure that the child's safety and best interests are kept at the forefront of the assessment.

- The assessment may need to explore sensitive issues around disability, culture, ethnicity, religion and sexual orientation, and the impact of these factors on the task of caring for a child. Social workers must ensure that prospective carers understand why this must be done to ensure an open and honest exchange. To do this effectively, skilled professionals require supervision and time for analysis and reflection. Organisations must recognise the importance of providing support and training for supervisors and appropriate resources.

- The information gathered during the assessment was not always subject to critical appraisal and effective analysis. Additionally, the fostering and adoption panels did not always exercise sufficient scrutiny or challenge of the information provided during the approval process.

- Professional differences of opinion about prospective carers are bound to occur both within and between agencies, and across different disciplines. If these are dismissed or denied, it can result in inadequate assessments that may have tragic consequences. An open discussion is a valuable way of gaining a greater understanding of the applicants and triangulating information.

- A further assessment of foster carers, or adopters of additional children, takes place when carers seek to change the status of a resident child, or move to a different local authority or to an independent fostering provider. In some cases, this assessment was cursory and incomplete, and represented a missed opportunity to explore the suitability of the carers. There are very different perspectives on this current process. Experienced carers and some professionals argue for a lighter touch or modified assessment, which contrasts with many of the reviews in the current study that called for greater rigour.

- Special guardianship orders are increasingly used to provide care for looked after children, driven by the view that "family is best". They were intended to complement adoption – an option for older children who have an existing relationship with the family or family friends. There were concerns raised over the assessment of special guardians in each of the six cases included in this study. A key issue was the 26-week statutory timeframe (in England and Wales), because it could result in rushed assessments and premature decisions. This was of particular concern as the children were predominantly very young, and half had never lived with or had a relationship with the proposed special guardian.

- Special guardianship as the preferred permanence option, regardless of the circumstances, influenced assessment decisions. It led to superficial assessments that lacked rigour and either ignored or were over-optimistic about identified areas of concern. This was particularly evident when proposed carers were already well known to children's social care.

- There was an over-reliance on the information provided by the potential special guardians, which was neither checked nor supplemented with information from other sources. Referees were not always interviewed and too much credence was given to their written submissions. When checks were sought, the 26-week timeframe (in England and Wales) could result in them not being completed in time for the court hearing.

- Once the courts grant a special guardianship order, children cease to be looked after, children's social care usually close the case, and existing plans for looked after children are terminated. The assessment must explore how best to support prospective special guardians to ensure that the child's best interests are met and plans are in place to support these children through the major life changes they will experience.

Chapter 4
Children at the heart of practice

In all actions concerning children, whether undertaken by public or private social welfare institutions, courts of law, administrative authorities or legislative bodies, the best interests of the child shall be a primary consideration.

(United Nations Convention on the Rights of the Child, 1990, p.4, Article 3(1))

WHO ARE THE 98 CHILDREN IN THE STUDY?

The 52 case reviews related to 98 children. Before exploring what insights the findings provide on how best to keep children at the heart of professional practice, it is important to understand who they are.

The child's background

Not all of the serious case reviews recorded the children's histories or the reasons why they first became looked after. This information was rarely found in historical cases of sexual abuse, or reviews with a specific focus such as home education. Where information is available, it suggests that children's social care were involved with the child's family prior to placement. There were two exceptions: an instance of private fostering and a case of an unaccompanied child asylum seeker.

The child's age when first placed away from home was recorded for 53 of the 98 children: the majority (64%) had been under five when they left the care of their parents. Twenty-one children had been with their parents for less than a year and another 13 had been removed from home between the ages of one and five years. The numbers diminished, as children got older: ten were removed in middle childhood (6-10 years), eight between the ages of 11 and 15, and one child was 17 years old when arriving in England.

Most of the children had had a turbulent start to life. Many had grown up in families that lived in poverty, experienced poor parental mental health, learning disability, drug and alcohol misuse and domestic abuse;

issues also identified in the triennial analysis carried out by Brandon and colleagues (2020). The children had suffered abuse and neglect while living with their birth parents. The following case provides an insight into the early life of Child R, a 15-year-old girl.

> *R was the main target of her mother's abuse, which included emotional rejection and physical assaults. She was neglected and left in charge of her younger siblings; she was exposed to many adults who could have posed a risk to her. R was made the subject of a Child Protection (CP) Plan in 2009. She ran away early in 2010 [aged nine years] asking to be taken into care because her mother had beaten her. Her siblings were removed shortly after this, and all the children have been looked after under care orders from that point onwards.*

Frequent moves, multiple losses, experiences of rejection during childhood and the lack of a significant attachment figure will have a devastating impact on a child. Children will be left feeling unwanted, unacceptable and that they are outsiders. The review relating to YP1, a 13-year-old girl, is sadly an illustration of this. She had been placed in foster care due to increasing concerns about her home life, family rejection, substance misuse, episodes of going missing, suicidal ideation, and sexual exploitation. Little changed in this girl's unhappy life after placement, and a few months after going to live with these foster carers, she died at a party of a drug overdose.

There were, however, a few cases where there had been no child protection concerns. Two reviews related to children who became looked after because their mother, a single parent, had died. In two other cases, the review related to asylum seekers: one focused on the child of a failed asylum seeker who had been given to friends when she returned to her country of origin; the other was the very distressing case of an unaccompanied child who had sought asylum in the UK.

> *An unaccompanied asylum seeking child (UASC) presenting as a 17-year-old male from Eritrea first came to their notice following his arrest in...London on 8 July 2016. After initial assessment and investigation of his situation, he was placed under "Police Protection" and looked after in emergency foster care commissioned by...Children's Social Care Emergency Duty Team (EDT). The following evening (9 July 2016), at approximately 9pm YT was found by his foster carers hanging in his bedroom. He was dead. The circumstances indicated that the death was a suicide.*

FACTORS AFFECTING PLACEMENT CHOICE

> *Fostering services must ensure that the welfare, safety and individual needs of looked after children are central to the care provided by foster*

carers, so that each looked after child is treated as an individual and given personal support tailored to their individual needs, and taking their wishes and feelings fully into account.

(HM Government, 2011, p.11, para 2.3)

When a decision is made to remove children from the care of their parents, social workers are faced with identifying the best arrangement to meet the needs of the child. Successful matching depends on making a good assessment, high levels of information sharing and careful decision-making. The strongest potential matches are based on ensuring that the parenting capacity, skills and experience of the carer meet the assessed developmental needs of the child.

The role of funding

Recent cuts to local authority funding have had a negative impact on the resources available to children's social care when placing a child.

We heard about a system at breaking point, increasingly reliant on the goodwill of social care professionals; the children supported by or in the care of councils are some of the most vulnerable in society and deserve better.

(House of Commons Housing, Communities and Local Government Committee, 2019, p.3)

To control costs, local authorities may seek to place children with their own foster carers – "in house placements". Although the overwhelming majority of children needing a foster placement are placed, there is a shortage of carers who can look after children exhibiting disturbing behaviour.

This means that, too often, matches are made between carers and children that are not ideal and, after a short period, the child has to be moved again.

(Narey and Owers, 2018, p.12)

The consequence of placing a disturbed and distressed child with carers who do not have the relevant skills was highlighted in a review relating to R, a 15-year-old young person. Her turbulent and abusive history had resulted in poor mental health and accompanying behavioural difficulties, with a pattern of going missing. As a result, placements often did not last and the review recorded how this impacted on her subsequent life. The girl had come into care aged 10, and four years later she had experienced seven placements (plus two respite placements). A key issue identified in the review was a failure to read or understand the girl's history, along with a number of contributing factors, including information that had been archived, no electronic system for children's files, and over-stretched staff.

As a result, R's psycho-social history, her own and her family's experiences, and the degree and nature of her vulnerability (including to child sexual exploitation) were poorly understood by those acting as her "corporate parent", as well as by their multi-agency partners.

This affected plans and decision-making, which in many instances appeared to be reactive rather than considered and based on knowledge of R's complex needs...In terms of wider planning, a clear and pro-active approach to R's placements was lacking, as most of these were unplanned and appeared to rely on "what was available at the time".

They suggest that some of R's carers were not suitable to meet her needs, but were likely chosen because they were the only local resource available when the previous placement disrupted.

The review noted how R's needs appeared to have taken second place to the availability of placements.

Some reviews identified how the necessity to control costs could influence the choice of carers. This reflects the DfE (2014) finding that too many children coming into care because of abuse and neglect were not getting the right placements the first time around.

Local authorities often base decisions on children's placements on short-term affordability rather than on plans to best meet the child's needs.

(DfE, 2014, p.9, para 12)

This emphasis on affordability is highlighted in the review relating to eight-year-old Claire. She was well known to children's social care, having experienced neglect and sexual abuse while living with her birth mother. The care plan was for long-term fostering. In this local authority, the Business Relationship Team was responsible for identifying resources for child placements. The review team found that:

...there are two distinct processes in place in placement decision making, one that makes decisions about where a child should be placed based primarily on resource availability and cost, and one that is a practice-based decision-making process that matches a child to placement based on a child's needs. There was a divergence of views amongst staff members from the different teams about where matching a child's needs to carers takes place.

The review found that this confusion generated tensions between the different staff teams:

I have often got frustrated that people were putting resources rather than the child's needs first (front line practitioner)...*You have to take what you are given...there is no choice* (case group member)...*it is pot luck what is the budget available, and what is available on the day* (manager).

Fifteen months after Claire went to live with her foster carers, Mr and Mrs George, she was removed from the placement, having contracted gonorrhoea and chlamydia.

The role of independent fostering providers

The lack of sufficient local authority foster placements has resulted in greater use of independent fostering providers (IFPs) (Baginsky et al, 2017). The DfE's 2018 review of foster care in England suggested that local authorities were using these services for about one-third of their placements in 2016–17 (Narey and Owers, 2018).

Although a placement through an IFP may be considerably more expensive than an in-house placement, some provide foster carers with the necessary skills to look after children with complex needs. This was evident in 11 reviews where an IFP had been responsible for the placement of 19 children. Of these, eight were older (10 years or more), six belonged to a minority ethnic group, and three had identified mental health problems.

Moreover, although the review of foster placements undertaken for the DfE found no discernible difference in the quality of care offered by local authorities and that offered by IFPs, foster carers reported being 'more satisfied with supervising social worker support from independent agencies' (Narey and Owers, 2018, p.60).

The findings from the reviews suggest that dependence on IFPs may result in confusion over roles and responsibilities. This was shown in the case of Child A, a 17-year-old boy who had been placed in care at the age of three years as a result of significant abuse and neglect. The foster carers subsequently adopted him. At the age of nine, Child A had been assessed as unable to cope in mainstream school and identified as having attention deficit hyperactivity disorder (ADHD) with behaviour described as aggressive and very challenging. A year later the family situation had broken down and Child A was accommodated by the local authority, under section 20, and placed with 'very supportive foster carers'.

Child A had become very anxious about leaving care and had consistently told the professionals around him of his fears. Just before his 18th birthday Child A killed himself:

> At the time of his death Child A was living with his foster carers where he had been for almost four years. This was a commissioned independent foster placement.

The review identified shortcomings in management decision-making and reported on the lack of management oversight from the children's social work service. It went on to note:

The approach adopted by independent foster care agency of Team Parenting was particularly strong; however, the inconsistent participation of the right partners in the process resulted in a confused demarcation of professional roles and accountability. The practice was therefore well meaning but missed the opportunity to have greater impact on positive outcomes for Child A.

The confusion over roles and responsibilities was similarly highlighted in the review relating to Child J, a 12-year-old Black girl (ethnicity described in the review in these terms). This girl had a long history of self-harm, severe depression and suicidal ideation. Her life was chaotic and unsettled, with frequent moves between home, grandparents and foster care. J spent several months as an in-patient in a specialist adolescent psychiatric unit, because of her self-harming and possible suicide, before being placed with new foster carers. The review noted that, unlike the preparation for J's first foster placement, where 'good risk assessments were undertaken and reviewed to mitigate against dangers of hanging, cutting or ingestion', this had not been carried out:

... such written risk assessments of the environment were not put in place by the placing authority on the un-checked assumption that the independent foster agency would do this.'

Child J took her own life at the age of 14 years.

The evidence from the reviews highlights the importance of clear lines of communication when more than one agency is involved, regardless of whether it is a local authority or independently provided.

Pressures to increase the numbers of children placed in the same household

The pressures in fostering services may result in social workers placing more children in the household than foster carers have been approved to look after (Brazier, 2019).

The case of Child V serves as an illustration. The review recorded that the decision to place this baby girl with foster carers exceeded the number of children that the carers had been approved to look after. The placement was agreed, subject to increased monitoring and support for the carers. However, the review noted: 'Overall, there is no evidence of extra support being provided'. Aged three months, Child V was taken to hospital and 'died with evidence of non-accidental injuries but the cause of death points to a rare cause not related to the non-accidental injuries'.

Another case shows how staff and managers, through "innovative" interpretations, may justify not adhering to the regulations. The review dealing with carers who had fostered over 30 children, many for short periods, often exceeding the number whom they were approved to look after, illustrates this point.

One member of staff reported that it had been acceptable to treat a sibling group of three as "one placement" rather than three children.

This review went on to show how other flexible ways had been used to interpret regulations. It noted that the service manager justified the placement of more than the agreed number of children because he 'felt that there was sometimes a pragmatic need to adopt a more permissive reading of the regulations'. His reasons included the financial pressures 'to use in-house foster carers and not agencies' in placing children, and the possibility to 'use some fostering placements creatively because there were some good foster carers who "could cope".' The male foster carer in this case was convicted of more than 20 sexual offences against five foster children in his care.

Lack of a clear proactive approach

The findings from the case reviews suggest that placements are often unplanned or rely on what is available. A number of the serious case reviews noted that children were placed with undue haste; a factor identified in relation to all types of permanent care. The case of three siblings placed for adoption serves as an example.

The placement introductions were carried out with indecent haste and were not child-focused, and not evaluated sufficiently.

The siblings remained with their adopters for nine years before the frequent episodes of physical abuse, neglect and emotional abuse were identified.

Similar issues were raised in the review relating to the placement of children with the foster carers CF and IW. The inquiry report drew attention to the finding that, when deciding on making a placement, the child's individual needs were not always the paramount focus of decision-making.

The early placements of children with CF and IW were made either to provide CF and IW with initial experiences of fostering in practice or to meet the needs of other foster carers for short-term respite from caring longer-term for certain children. Placements were not made in order to meet the assessed and planned needs of individual children and matched with the capabilities of CF and IW.

In the discussion of issues surrounding special guardianship in the previous chapter, it was evident that the statutory requirement in England and Wales to complete proceedings within 26 weeks allowed little time for preparing the child and family. In the following two cases, prior to placement the child had neither lived with the potential special guardians nor knew them.

The first example relates to a four-year-old girl where the mother's poor mental health meant that she could not look after her daughter. The girl had initially been placed in foster care and care proceedings had been initiated. A paternal aunt had been identified as a potential special guardian, although she did not know the child at the time, having met the girl only on one occasion. The review commented on the transition process:

> The transition planning process for Child J should have been more detailed given that this was a completely new relationship and the needs of Child J were complex. However, there is no expectation of a fuller transition plan in the context of the special guardianship process.

Fundamental to the difficulties with the planning process was that J's views about the potential move had not been taken into consideration, being 'thought to be too young to understand the process'. This was in spite of her having expressed her desire to go home and her confusion over where she would be living in the future. Sadly, J was found dead at the age of eight at the home of her paternal aunt; her aunt and paternal grandmother were both found guilty of child cruelty.

The case of LH, a four-year-old boy placed with his maternal aunt, is another example of the lack of adequate preparation when looked after children are placed with potential special guardians:

> As such there was no "lead in" time or much preparation time for Child LH and he was placed almost straight away after proceedings ended.

The maternal aunt was found to have physically abused this young boy.

Inadequate placement planning

The following two cases illustrate the fatal consequences that can occur when very young children are placed without adequate assessment and planning. The first relates to a baby boy, born at home following a concealed pregnancy. The initial hospital admission identified complex health needs. The baby had been discharged after three weeks without any assessment or initial child protection conference, and placed with the foster carers who were looking after the baby's half-sibling. The Independent Reviewing Officer (IRO) thought that this was an administrative decision, rather than based on an analysis of how best to meet this baby's needs. Sadly, the baby died aged nine weeks; the post-mortem revealed multiple rib fractures.

The second case also concerns a baby boy. Taken by his mother to the hospital on two occasions with non-accidental injuries, during his first month of life, an emergency placement had been made with foster carers. At the time, there was a requirement in the local authority for social workers to explore all options for "in house" foster placements.

Child T was placed in spite of the close age of other children in the placement. He was admitted straight from hospital with no placement meeting, and the Placement Plan was drafted in the children's social care office and not in the carers' home with their involvement. No social worker accompanied the child to the foster home...This did not comply with placement guidelines and was not good practice.

Four months later the child died; the foster mother pleaded guilty to manslaughter.

A lack of planning was not confined to the placement of very young children. This was illustrated in the inquiry report of same-sex male foster carers, CF and IW, who had sexually abused some 18 children. Their first placement was that of 'a child who was at the upper age limit of their terms of approval, with a continuing history of problematic, inappropriate sexualised behaviour'. This placement was made despite the fostering social worker having noted in the assessment report, and confirmed by the panel minutes, that 'I would not be looking to place a child who was publicly demonstrating overtly sexualised behaviour'. The review noted that the lack of planning or assessment in the matching process about any risk this child may have presented to other resident children, or them to him, was repeated with regard to a number of other children subsequently placed with these foster carers. CF and IW were both convicted on several counts of sexual activity with a child.

When placements are carried out with undue haste, it can leave children feeling disoriented and frightened. Children may not understand why they have been removed from their parents or current carers and blame themselves for the move. In one case, a girl of 14 years with a 'very poor psycho-social history' had a background of self-harm and suicidal ideation. Following the death of her mother, she had lived with her aunt. Her diary at this time (aged 13 years) revealed 'feeling unwanted, low self-esteem...' Her aunt had experienced difficulties in looking after her and it had been agreed by children's social care that she should be accommodated. The girl noted in her diary that she felt rejected and hurt on moving from her aunt. The aunt also told the review that 'she had learned of the planned move by text and packed J's belongings for the same evening. J did not say goodbye to her.'

A lack of adequate planning continued to follow this girl. After a period as an inpatient in a psychiatric unit, she had been placed with new foster carers.

Whilst it is understood the foster mother was told of the risks, she did not understand the seriousness of these risks and the risks were not sufficiently articulated in a risk management plan. The lack of a risk assessment was critical. It is unclear how decisions could be made, in relation to whether carers are able to keep J safe, without a risk assessment. J was being discharged with no effective treatment in place to address her long-standing depression and no follow-up secured.

Ignoring parental wishes

A special guardian is usually someone with a close relationship to the child, such as a family member, former foster carer or family friend.

(CoramBAAF, 2015)

Unlike adoption, the order retains a basic legal link with birth parents. They remain legally the child's parents, though their ability to exercise their parental responsibility is limited.

(DfE, 2017a, p.8, para 12)

When children living with their birth parents are moved to the care of a special guardian, there might be an expectation that birth parents' views on the applicants would be taken into consideration. When there is no existing relationship between the potential special guardian and the child, the birth parents' views may provide important information for social workers when assessing whether the placement would be in the child's best interest.

In two of the reviews, it was noted that the birth mother had expressed strong concerns about the proposed placement, expressly asking for her child not to be placed with the identified relative. In both cases, the mothers' concerns were not taken into consideration at the point at which the suitability of the special guardian was assessed.

The review of a baby girl of White British and Black African background, who had been cared for by a distant relative on a special guardianship order, is one example: 'The mother had specifically stated that she did not want her child to be cared for by any of her extended family'. The mother's contribution to the review process highlights how her views were disregarded.

The mother knew little about the court case but she was spoken to, and she said to them quite clearly that she did not want Shi-Anne to go to Kandyce Downer at any time. This was because of how she is with her own children. She feels that her wishes should've been heard but they weren't…She did object to the name change and told her solicitor this, but it happened anyway.

The guidance is clear that when a special guardianship order is in force, written consent of the parent or the leave of the court must be given if the child is to be known by a different surname (DfE, 2017a).

The other example relates to a Black African-Caribbean boy of four years, whose mother had a learning disability. There was a child protection plan for neglect, and the maternal aunt was assessed to see if she could provide the boy with a safe and caring environment. The child had begun living with the maternal aunt, who had put herself forward to be his special guardian, without sufficient preparation. During the full special guardianship order assessment, children's social care had received a letter from the boy's mother about her sister, in which she had 'explicitly refused consent for her to be the carer for any of her children'.

The boy's mother, accompanied by an Intermediary who knew her well, met with the reviewers. The Intermediary assisted the reviewers to speak to the mother in a way that enabled her to contribute fully. At this meeting, the boy's mother reinforced her disagreement with the arrangement, saying that 'she was opposed to this and talked about the letter that she had written to the social worker to state that she did not want this'.

The regulations relating to special guardianship orders state that the assessment should consider the impact that an order would have on the existing relationship between the prospective special guardian, the child and the parent (UK Statutory Instruments, 2005; DfE, 2017a). The outcome in both the above cases was tragic. Shi-Anne died as a result of non-accidental injuries inflicted by her special guardian: 'The post-mortem revealed over 150 injuries both internal and external that had been caused over a number of months'. In the other case, the little boy survived; the review identified that he had also suffered serious injuries at the hand of the special guardian, his maternal aunt.

These findings suggest that greater weight should be given to the opposition birth parents may raise to a potential special guardian. Such objections need to be recorded in the social worker's report and inform the special guardianship assessment. The rights of parents with learning disabilities or where English is not their first language to have equal access to statutory processes such as court proceedings is essential. Many will need to be supported by advocacy or other media to enable them to play as full a part as possible in the proceedings.

Placing very vulnerable children in the same household

Many children who are fostered, adopted or who live with special guardians will have suffered long-term abuse and neglect. The stress experienced by children exposed to multi-type abuse has consequences that are more difficult to reverse than exposure to single-type abuse (Sesar *et al*, 2010). To cope with their situation, children learn to behave in particular ways. Such coping mechanisms, which may be advantageous in abusive situations, can have the opposite effect when the child's situation changes. When placing very vulnerable children together in the same household, social workers should always consider the possible impact they can have on one another. The reviews suggest that when exploring possible placements, assessment and matching did not always take this into account.

A review that focused on the 'sexually harmful behaviour between adolescent males and the sexual abuse of a younger boy in a local authority foster placement' serves as an example. All four boys had been removed from their homes as a result of abuse, neglect and exposure to sexual violence and placed with the same foster carers. Prior to placement, each boy had a history of sexual behaviour with a younger child.

> *The decision to place four vulnerable children together was not the result of a considered understanding of the dynamics of the placement. John may be considered as the resident child; in the sense that this was the only placement he had known, and he had been with the carers the longest. The other children were added incrementally...*

The review noted that 'John was known to have a long-standing history of sexualised behaviour; a level of sexual knowledge and an interest disproportionate to his chronological age'. John had a diagnosis of Asperger's syndrome. It had been assumed that his interest lay in young girls and that boys would not have been at risk; while still living at home his younger sister had disclosed that he had sexually abused her. It was reported that John and another adolescent boy in the foster home 'may have engaged in mutual sexual behaviour during the time they were placed together'. These two boys were found to have sexually abused nine-year-old Christopher who was also fostered with this family.

Another example of placing very vulnerable children within the same household without sufficient assessment and planning is shown in the case of a young girl. Born with kidney problems that required ongoing medical attention, at the age of nine she had been adopted into a household that included three older adopted boys. Six months later, she had been admitted to hospital 'with multiple stab wounds to her chest, abdomen and arms...Her condition required intensive care and surgery'. Her adopted brother, aged 16 years (a boy with cerebral palsy and complex needs) was charged and convicted of the assault. The review suggests that the possible impact of placing more than one child with complex needs in the same household had not been fully explored.

The findings from the following review also highlight the negative consequences of not assessing the possible impact of placing very vulnerable young people together. This very different scenario featured two teenage mothers and their babies living in the same foster home. Both mothers had suffered childhood abuse, had low self-esteem, self-harmed, and exhibited challenging behaviours. The review considered that the placement would have had the ability to provide the support and help that was needed for either of the young women, but not for both at the same time.

The lack of any consideration of the joint placement by the relevant social workers and other professionals was a significant omission.

The outcome was tragic. Aged six weeks, one of the babies was admitted to hospital, critically ill due to suspected salt poisoning. The court concluded that 'the overwhelming likelihood was that another young mother in the same foster placement was responsible for contaminating his feed'.

In other cases, although the outcome may not have been as heart-breaking, nonetheless the importance of considering other children within the household when planning a placement was emphasised.

The review has underlined the importance of ensuring that SGO placements are supported by a robust plan that is tailored to the individual needs of the children (including any children who are existing members of the household) and their potential carers.

A conveyor belt approach to placements

When foster carers provide a variety of placements, understanding what is happening to individual children can be difficult. Changes in their behaviour may not be identified or linked to their time with these particular carers. The sample of serious case reviews included three historical cases involving numerous children who had been sexually abused by their male foster carer. The difficulty in identifying problems had been exacerbated by the high throughput of children. The carers in the following example provided short-term and respite placements and some of the children had complex needs.

The large numbers of children placed with FC1 and FC2 over the years meant that co-ordination of information about the behaviours of children with the details of carers was not routine; in other words, the changed behaviour of some of the children could not be easily linked with specific placement and therefore patterns could not be discerned...

A report by the Independent Inquiry into Child Sexual Abuse (2019) includes the case of foster carers FC1 and FC2 in its investigation. It noted that:

Gallagher (FC1) pleaded guilty to 55 sexual offences, including rape, committed against 16 boys between 1998 and 2010. Gallagher received 13 life sentences and was to serve at least 28 years. He abused young boys on an "unprecedented scale" and did "incalculable" damage. None of the abuse was detected over this 12-year period.

(Independent Inquiry into Child Sexual Abuse, 2019, p.88, para 5.13)

The impact of a high throughput of children on understanding what happens in fostering households was also evident in historical cases where children had suffered other forms of abuse and neglect. A baby girl born with neonatal abstinence syndrome had spent 34 days in hospital before being placed with foster carers. These carers had looked after 14 children under the age of three years, placements that were often short-term and which were all task-focused. At the time at which the baby had been placed with them, there was a litany of concerns about the carers, including: an allegation of physical assault, five occasions when a child was not taken for health appointments, a failure to pick up on children's illnesses, and four children in their care who experienced faltering growth. In addition, it was noted that they lacked warmth or interest in the children in their care.

When there is no chronology of incidents or concerns about the foster carers, children could be at risk of abuse and neglect. For this baby, it was to prove disastrous: 'After discharge [from hospital], Child V spent 51 days living with the couple until her death'.

Large groups of children

A related issue that can obscure what is happening in the household is when numerous children live in the same home. Nearly one-third (31%) of the reviews related to more than one child living in the household. High numbers do not necessarily mean that social workers are placing more children than carers have been registered to look after, as one review noted.

> The law provides that there should be a usual limit of three foster children placed by a local authority in a household...Children adopted by carers and any children of their own that they may have are not included.

A three-year-old girl and her brother, aged six years, had suffered abuse and neglect prior to being fostered. Seven years after placement, the little girl's brother told his teacher that he had seen his then 10-year-old sister being sexually abused by the 19-year-old adopted son of their carer.

When the little girl and her brother had come to live in the foster home, the household contained two birth children, an adopted daughter and three foster children, later to be adopted. During the seven years they were there, a further nine children arrived, three permanently and others on a short-term basis. The review acknowledged that exemptions had been granted to allow more than three foster children to be looked after by the carer, but 'found no evidence that a careful assessment was undertaken of the needs of each individual child within the household and the likely impact on the welfare of each child, including the perpetrator, as expected by the regulations and guidance'.

CHILDREN'S EXPERIENCE OF THE CARE SYSTEM

Information available from the the reviews suggests that some two-thirds of the children had spent long periods in substitute care before their abuse and neglect was recognised. For others, the period was short; 16 (32%) had been separated from their parents for less than a year. Tragically, for 13 of the 16 children, their placement was to prove fatal. For a few of the children who had died, the review showed that the outcome was clearly out of the hands of practitioners, as was the case of the unaccompanied asylum-seeking child who had committed suicide the day after he was placed with foster carers.

For the children who had spent years away from home in substitute care before their abuse had been identified, 14 (28%) had lived for eight years or more in abusive alternative households. For many, life was turbulent after separating from their birth parents. Child R, the 15-year-old girl who had asked to be taken into care at the age of nine years, serves to illustrate a care experience that was not uncommon for children in the current study. In her case, she spent two unstable years living away from home before being raped at the age of 15 years by an unknown man.

> R has had an unsettled time in terms of placements, experiencing eight moves in care. There was a stable placement (spring 2010 to late summer 2011), which was followed by a period of highly unsettled behaviour and placement disruptions. In addition, R has now had a total of ten allocated social workers.

Barriers to understanding the child's world

To understand a child's world, it is essential to see it through their eyes and to listen to their views, wishes and feelings. The UN Convention on the Rights of the Child (1990, Article 12) is clear that children have a right to express their views and feelings on matters that affect them, and that these should be taken seriously.

Social workers need to use their skills sensitively and creatively in order to understand what is happening to children, and this is only possible when visits are undertaken regularly. Government guidance and regulations state that the child's social worker must visit the child in their foster home within a week of the start of the placement, and that subsequent visits must take place at intervals of no more than six weeks. Placements that are intended to last until the child is 18 must be visited every three months after the first year (HM Government, 2010a).

A carousel of social workers

The reviews suggested that, although local authorities tried to ensure that social workers visited children at the required intervals, a shortage of resources, overwhelming caseloads and many changes of social worker due to high staff turnover may result in the child's voice not being heard. The increasing pressures on social workers were acknowledged by the House of Commons Select Committee Report (2019).

> A respondent to our survey said that 'the system would collapse if it wasn't for the goodwill of practitioners going above and beyond because of their values and not wanting to let kids down'. We heard that this was leading to difficulties in recruiting children's social workers.

> (House of Commons Housing, Communities and Local Government, 2019, p.46, para 116)

Visiting and observing babies and very young children is essential, because they have no capacity to voice their distress. Child T, a baby who had been placed with foster carers at the age of 20 months, was admitted to hospital three months later as an emergency with non-accidental injuries. The review highlighted the dangers that can occur when social work oversight is not adequate.

> The transfer of the case at a number of key practice points (as part of the organisational structure in place in children's social care at that time) led to a situation where no one social worker had overall personal knowledge of Child T.

A lack of resources and time

The negative impact of unmanageable workloads was illustrated in a case of historic serial sexual abuse. In discussing the supervision of the children, the review noted that overworked social workers prioritised 'court work or local authority and multi-agency procedures'. This consuming and challenging work distracted 'attention from the task of visiting children, seeing them alone and developing a detailed understanding of their experience in the current placement'.

However, simply visiting children in line with statutory requirements will not necessarily enable children to talk freely. Abused children most often confide in adults with whom they have built a close and trusting relationship. Faced with the current workloads, social workers find this difficult to achieve. Without such a relationship, children rarely talk about the most difficult issues in their lives. The review relating to the 10-year-old girl who had been sexually abused by the foster carers' adopted son illustrates how this can happen. In her contribution to the review, she discussed the factors that might have helped her to reveal her abuse to professionals.

> She said that she may have told a professional if she had had a better relationship with one, who had time, was really 'listening' and 'being genuine'. She thought professionals were 'rushed' and that they never asked questions more than once.

This lack of trust in professionals was found in many of the reviews, including that relating to a 15-year-old girl who had died as a result of inhaling butane gas.

> *Professionals struggled to establish a relationship with Child D that would have enabled her to accept support and to access relevant and age-appropriate service, for example, education.*

This meant that when the girl became pregnant, she felt unable to reveal who the father was. After her death, he was identified as a man more than twice her age.

In other instances, social workers may simply not "hear" what children are saying. The review relating to a 15-year-old boy illustrated how children's voices can be ignored. The boy had been accommodated at the age of eight years and had some 15 placements within the first three years. A period of stability followed, when he lived in a small independent sector children's home.

> *With the assistance from the Children's Rights section, he successfully resisted earlier attempts to move him to foster placements nearer his family. When he was almost 15, still clearly against his better judgement and expressed wishes, he moved to a foster family with the intention that this would provide him with a good experience of family life up to the age of 18.*

The placement did not work out and he had soon been moved to a second foster home where another 15-year-old boy with a serious drug habit had joined him. The boys had not got on. Following a disagreement with his carer, the boy had gone missing and in the early hours of the morning had been found dead due to an overdose of drugs.

When children have communication or learning difficulties, their views are more difficult to elicit and more easily ignored, as the following case illustrates. A 14-year-old boy with ADHD and Asperger's Syndrome had been sexually abused when placed for respite care in the foster household of two male carers. The children's social worker 'asked Child P whether he enjoyed respite with CF and IW to which Child P said no'. The social worker 'did not pursue this further with Child P'.

Children's fear of disclosure

Sexual abuse can have long-term consequences for children's mental health and social functioning and lead to dissociation and memory impairment (NSPCC, 2013), blocking possible disclosure. The investigative report by the Independent Inquiry into Child Sexual Abuse (2019) outlines the barriers children face to disclosing their abuse during childhood. Many of these were evident in the reviews included in the current study.

Children feared retributive violence or being separated from family. As a consequence, the abuse may only be revealed once the child has left the household. In some cases, children remained silent about the harm they were experiencing until they reached adulthood, years after leaving their abuser. The abuse of five adopted children only came to light once the eldest, aged 20 years, felt safe:

> In December 2004, Belinda left home as a young adult, she made allegations that she and the other children had been consistently physically and emotionally abused by Mrs Spry, by being beaten with implements or punched, locked in their bedrooms and starved of food. Belinda also complained that Mrs Spry had forced her to remain as a wheelchair user.

Of particular relevance was the fear of not being believed, or being told by the perpetrator that they would not be believed. For example, the children's interviews in the review relating to a perpetrator of sexual abuse against girls illustrate the power that carers can wield in influencing a child's perceptions:

> The children in the household had been told by Mr F that social workers were "bad" and would take them away. In these circumstances they were fearful of talking to social workers.

When children have experienced apparent kindness and attention from their foster carer, they may have conflicted feelings about disclosing what is happening to them (Independent Inquiry into Child Sexual Abuse, 2019). For example, a 12-year-old boy had lived with two different single male foster carers, both of whom had sexually abused him, prior to weekly boarding at a residential school. He had frequently run away from school to return to his second foster carer:

> Child PB again was reported missing and police call at home of FC2. FC2 denied he had seen PB. Police find PB hiding undressed in wardrobe.

The review noted that there appeared to be an agreed "pact" between the foster carer and the boy 'not to say anything'.

Other fears may keep children silent. For example, the shame associated with cultural norms of masculinity can impact on boys' willingness to discuss their abuse (Evans, 2019). This was an issue identified in a review relating to a serial sex abuser of young boys. The report suggested that boys might be reluctant to reveal their abuse because of 'a fear of being branded as "gay" or feeling un-masculine'.

Children with disabilities experience additional barriers to disclosing abuse (Frederick et al, 2019). They may have inadequate language to describe their abuse, not discern what is happening to them, or fail to understand that the behaviour is abusive.

A seven-year-old girl had developmental delay, mild learning disabilities and delayed motor skills and co-ordination. Her mother's poor mental health had resulted in her, aged four years, being placed with foster carers before going to live with her paternal aunt on a special guardianship order. The girl's behaviour had quickly showed signs of serious disturbance. However, her aunt had ensured that the focus was deflected from her parenting by blaming the girl. Her aunt had explained bruises, burns and cuts as incidents of self-harming. The review noted that this was generally accepted and practitioners failed to understand the girl's situation.

> The issue of Child J's potential self-harming behaviour was not questioned, and more thought should have been given to either reflecting on the likelihood of this level of self-harm in a six-year-old and therefore concern about her well-being.

The girl was found dead at the age of seven years, at the home where she lived with her aunt. The aunt was found guilty of child cruelty.

Independent visitors

The serious case reviews showed that many children who had experienced abuse and neglect from the very people who should have been protecting them had no one to whom they could turn for help or advice. To overcome the barriers children face in revealing their situation, they need a consistent, trusted adult to act as their champion and mentor.

An independent visitor is someone who has the duty of visiting, advising and befriending a looked after child (Schedule 2, Children Act 1989). The local authority can appoint an independent visitor when a looked after child has little or no communication with parents or those with parental responsibility and it is deemed to be in the child's best interest. The child must be in agreement with the decision. The appointment of an independent visitor should be considered at the development of a care plan or as part of a review of the child's case:

> An independent visitor is a volunteer who doesn't work for social care services, and is there to visit and befriend the child. Independent visitors need to be consistent and reliable in order that children can build a trusting, positive relationship with them over time. They will endeavour to become and remain a consistent adult in the child's life who doesn't change when placements or social workers change and will at all times stay child-focused.

(Gordon and Graham, 2016, p.3)

A Freedom of Information request in 2015 found that only 3.2 per cent of the total looked after children population in England were matched with an independent visitor (Gordon and Graham, 2016). None of the reviews included in the present study discussed the possibility of appointing an independent visitor at any point in the child's period in care. In only one case was this absence noted:

> *The possible appointment of an independent visitor was not addressed, despite paperwork highlighting the requirement being used when reviewing their cases.*

Research suggests that children and young people value their independent visitor particularly for the consistency of the relationship and the support they provide (Gordon and Graham, 2016). The potential for mentoring and befriending has been explored, and a key finding to its success is the involvement of the child or young person from the start of the decision-making process (Kersley and Estep, 2014).

SUMMARY OF KEY FINDINGS

- Most children in the study had a history of familial abuse and neglect that had resulted in their being removed from home at an early age. These early experiences may have a long-term impact on children's physical and mental health and their capacity to form attachment relationships. When children are placed away from home, it is vital that their needs are matched to the resources and abilities of carers. This depends on skilful and comprehensive assessment and review. Resources can influence the identification of the most appropriate placement. "In house" placements are seen to be more cost-effective than using an IFP. It is important that financial pressures do not result in the lowering of standards when placing children in foster homes.

- With increasing difficulties in recruiting foster carers, local authorities turn to independent providers to identify suitable carers, particularly for children with complex needs. The use of IFPs can lead to confusion and a lack of demarcation over professional roles and responsibilities and timely exchange of relevant information. This may result in issues that impact on a child's safety and welfare being missed or identified concerns not influencing the child's plan. Clarity over professional tasks and accountability is essential if children living away from home are to be kept safe from abuse and neglect.

- A lack of resources and over-worked professionals, in the cases studied, meant that Government guidance and regulations were not always strictly adhered to when matching a child's needs with the skills, qualities and experience of alternative carers. This was justified through interpreting the regulations in creative ways – bending the rules in this way can result in:

  - placements with carers who do not have the skills to look after a child with complex needs;

- placing more children than the foster carers are approved to look after;

- placements that support the needs of foster carers for respite rather than the needs of an individual child;

- a lack of planning prior to the placement.

● A failure to take a proactive approach to placements can lead to decisions being taken with undue haste. The consequences of this may be children not being adequately prepared, children's needs not being assessed, and a failure to understand the possible risks that a very disturbed child might present to other children in the household. Where children begin to live with special guardians, overly hurried arrangements can result from the requirement to complete proceedings within a court-directed timeframe.

● Special guardianship orders are usually granted to someone with a close relationship to the child. In the cases studied, the assumption of "family is best" appeared to negate the need to learn the child's views or to explore their existing relationship or attachment to the potential special guardian. Similarly, any concerns that the birth parent/s raised with professionals were not heard or were dismissed. When parents strongly oppose placement with the proposed special guardians, their views may have some validity. Parental objections should be recorded in the social worker's report, inform the assessment of the potential special guardian, and be made known to the court.

● When deciding on a placement, the assessment should focus on both the impact that a placement may have on resident children and its suitability for the child in question. Placing very vulnerable children together can result in them harming each other, both physically and sexually, or normalising self-harm and suicidal ideation.

● When there are multiples of children in emergency or temporary foster placements, this can obscure the abuse perpetrated by carers. To prevent this, assessments and reviews must collate and cross-check all concerning information and allegations made about the placement.

● There are numerous barriers to professionals' understanding of what is happening to children when they are living away from home. These include:

- a shortage of resources;

- ever-changing social workers;

- not prioritising time with the child;

- not listening to and considering children's views and wishes.

● The barriers to understanding a child's lived experience are frequently exacerbated because children do not easily discuss sensitive issues.

Children may not be able to speak about their abuse because they simply have no one in their lives whom they trust with such personal information. However, even when social workers visit regularly, children may be reluctant to speak about their abuse because they fear the consequences. They may fear not being believed; some are frightened of their carers; boys may fear that to admit having been sexually abused will affect their concept of self; other children may have conflicting emotions towards abusive carers who may also have shown them kindness.

- Children with disabilities have even greater difficulties in getting their voices heard. Practitioners must be aware that carers may deflect scrutiny of their abusive parenting by blaming a disabled child for their injuries. Particular attention must be taken to uncovering what life is like for these children.

- A significant number of children only feel confident enough to tell anyone about their abuse once they have left their foster home, adoptive family or special guardian. For some, this can mean surviving in an abusive household until adulthood, as some of the cases showed.

- No child included in the current sample had been matched with an independent visitor, reflecting the low use nationally. Independent visitors can provide a consistent adult able to mentor and champion the looked after child or young person. IROs should raise the possibility of appointing an independent visitor for the child at their review.

- In order to understand what life is like for a child, social workers must visit regularly and ensure that conversations are held in private. They need to spend time with the child so that a relationship of trust can develop. A variety of information should be used to build up a picture of what is going on in the household. This must be enhanced by what carers report. All the information, particularly when it relates to a child's disturbed behaviour, injuries or allegations, must be understood in the context of past history, discussions with other professionals, as well as observations and private conversations with the child.

Chapter 5
Support, oversight and review

When parents cannot provide a safe and stable environment for children, even with the support of the state, children can have their needs for a safe haven, offering love and stability, met through other means. The most frequent options for achieving permanent care are long-term fostering, child arrangements orders (previously known as residence orders), special guardianship orders, and adoption. Once a child is placed by the local authority, it is responsible for ensuring that Looked After Children (LAC) assessments and reviews are carried out.

The differences in the legal status of adopted or fostered children and those on special guardianship or child arrangements orders are reflected in the level of support and oversight children's social care provides to carers.

SUPPORTING FOSTER CARERS

Foster carers are part of the "team around the child", responsible for the safety and well-being of the child placed with them. A foster placement of a looked after child does not give parental responsibility to the carers; the local authority remains the child's "corporate parent".

All approved foster carers should undertake ongoing training and development, and it is the responsibility of fostering services to provide 'such training, advice, information and support, including outside office hours, as appears necessary in the interests of the children placed with them' (Fostering Services (England) Regulations 2011).

A supervising social worker should be assigned to the foster carers and meetings should be frequently held.

> Meetings have a clear purpose and provide the opportunity to supervise the foster carer's work, ensure the foster carer is meeting the child's needs, taking into account the child's wishes and feelings, and offer support and a framework to assess the carer's performance and develop their competencies and skills.

> (DfE, 2011, p.43, para 21.8)

A survey by the Fostering Network found that 70 per cent of foster carers felt that the support they received from their supervising social worker was excellent or good (Lawson and Cann, 2019). A similar level of satisfaction was found in some of the serious case reviews included in the present study, as illustrated by that of Child J:

The carers felt well supported. They had fostered for eleven years and know a number of staff in the independent agency – as some of them have previously been their link workers. Although they did not feel that they needed it, the agency rang every Monday to check how the weekend and previous week had gone for all the children.

The Lawson and Cann report (2019) suggests that foster carers do not always get the support they need from the child's placing authority.

Poor support from the child's placing authority – fewer than 40 per cent of respondents rated this as excellent or good – confirms what we hear all too often: that there is an ongoing disconnect between those with corporate parenting responsibility and the families with whom these children are placed.

(Lawson and Cann, 2019, p.14)

Although the initial foster carers for Child J had been satisfied with the support they received, later carers felt less well supported. Following an attempted suicide, the girl spent six months as an inpatient before being discharged to a new foster family. Confusion over which agency was responsible for providing the relevant specialist training, information and support was identified in the serious case review:

The foster family had no direct experience or training that covered working with inpatient mental health services or in caring for young people who had a recent history of depression/suicidal ideation and self-harm. This should have prompted a greater degree of support and guidance.

The review noted that there had been an assumption that 'this guidance should have been provided through the inpatient unit, this did not happen and the support provided to the foster carers by the fostering agency was inadequate'.

A lack of adequate support was highlighted in many of the reviews:

Once the children [a brother and sister] were placed, there is no evidence of any visits by the family placement social worker allocated to them despite the clear requirements...

A similar lack of appropriate support was identified in relation to the carers of a teenager. This adolescent girl had a long history of sexual abuse and bullying while living at home that resulted in self-harming behaviour, low self-esteem and suicidal ideation. Following numerous stays in an adolescent psychiatric unit, her first foster placement was with newly-approved carers:

The foster carers were inexperienced and it is apparent that little consideration was given to the ability of these foster carers to cope with the complexities of EW's emotions and behaviour and consideration of the well-being of their own children was not seen to be taken into account.

Foster carers, too, voiced their dissatisfaction with the level of support they received. The following quotation relates to a couple who had a birth child of two-and-a-half years and were fostering a young girl of 15 months. Their first language was not English.

The foster carers advised the lead reviewer that social workers often advised them about how busy they were and how little time they had. They said that whilst they accepted that this was the case, it made them feel as though no one had the time to listen to them.

Financial support

All foster carers receive a national weekly fostering allowance to cover the cost of caring for a child. The amount depends on where the carers live, the child's age and circumstances, and which local authority or independent service they foster with. Providing an allowance to enable and support families to foster a child is essential. However, the findings from the following review suggest that, when it becomes significant in the motivation to foster, children may not be safe from harm:

Financial difficulties are not necessarily an indicator of a safeguarding concern in a foster placement, however it was of particular significance in this case as their difficult financial circumstances proved to be a key part of the couple's motivation to foster children.

The issue of additional funding was also identified, in retrospect, by the reviews in relation to carers applying for a special guardianship order. One example is that of Shi-Anne, an 18-month-old girl placed with a distant relative and her four children:

The reason for this withdrawal [from her application to be Shi-Anne's special guardian] seemed to have been financial, as in addition to a weekly allowance, Kandyce Downer had requested a one-off payment of £3,500 to help her buy a car large enough for all the family. This request at this time had been refused. The review author feels that at this point the social worker and team manager should have been very concerned about Kandyce Downer's motivation for the SGO.

Another case involved a four-year-old boy placed with his aunt on a special guardianship order. Less than two months after taking on the care of the boy, the aunt had threatened to return him to the local authority 'due to what she described as "financial issues"'. The boy's mother had also raised concerns that the main reason her sister was offering to look after her child was financial.

PRIVATE FOSTERING ARRANGEMENTS

The Children (Private Arrangements or Fostering) Regulations 2005 and the National Minimum Standards for Private Fostering, issued under s.7 of the Local Authority Social Services Act 1970, form the legal framework governing private fostering in England (HM Government, 2005). The legislation places responsibility on the parent, carer and anyone else involved in making the private fostering arrangement to notify the local authority, six weeks before the arrangement is to begin.

Upon notification, local authorities are required, under the Children (Private Arrangements for Fostering) Regulations 2005, to visit the child and the private foster carers within seven days, to satisfy themselves that the welfare of the child is safeguarded and promoted. They must also check that the private foster carers are suitable and ensure that they have the information they need to help them to look after the child. If the arrangement is ongoing, the local authority must visit the child at least every six weeks during the first year and at least every 12 weeks thereafter. However, local authority support is clearly not possible if the authority has no knowledge of the private fostering arrangement. This may occur when families, for whatever reasons, wish to minimise their contact with authorities or have no knowledge of the regulations relating to looking after someone else's child.

The plight of a baby boy illustrates the importance of ensuring that parents and private foster carers can easily access information that sets out the requirement to inform the local authority. The baby's mother came from China on a student visa and gave birth when she was 17 years old. Mother and child had spent a short time in the care of a local authority before she claimed asylum and moved into accommodation provided by the asylum support service. When her asylum claim and subsequent appeal had been rejected, the mother removed herself and her child from all agencies previously involved. She placed her baby with a private foster carer, where he remained for a couple of months before another private carer assumed his care. The local authority had not been aware of these arrangements, and as a result no visits had been undertaken. Seven months after this child was separated from his mother, he was admitted to hospital 'not breathing, hypothermic and unresponsive'. The review highlighted the difficulties such circumstances present to local authorities in fulfilling their responsibilities to safeguard children from significant harm.

There was no information available in an appropriate language either to her or to the providers of the private fostering placements. Additionally both she and the private foster carers were unlikely to seek out local authority endorsement of the arrangements they had made.

SUPPORTING FAMILY AND FRIENDS OR KINSHIP CARERS

Family and friends care, or kinship care, is where a child, for whatever reason, goes to live with a relative, friend or other connected person. This may be a permanent arrangement, formalised through a legal order, or a temporary and informal one. The majority of kinship carers make an informal agreement with those holding parental responsibility for the children: 'Providing they are a relative of the child as defined by section 105 of the 1989 Act or have parental responsibility for the child, there is no requirement to notify the local authority of the arrangement' (DfE, 2010, p.14). In other circumstances, the arrangement may arise through the involvement of children's social care.

It is widely understood that, wherever possible, it is in the child's best interest to be brought up within the family. A placement with wider family members, however, will not necessarily guarantee a child's safety, particularly in families with an intergenerational history of abuse and neglect.

When a local authority is involved because the child is subject to a care order or s.20 arrangement in England and Wales under the Children Act 1989, or s.11 under the Children (Scotland) Act 1995, a formal assessment must be carried out. If approved to foster, kinship carers must receive the same support and supervision as any other foster carer.

Although the information relating to the child's past placements was not always available, eight of the serious case reviews noted that children had lived with, or were still living with, a relative at the time the harm had taken place. The findings from these reviews suggest a different attitude towards kinship carers: they were seen by children's social care as requiring less support because they knew the child and, as part of the family, had a moral obligation to provide care. The review relating to Claire, an eight-year-old girl, also suggested that family carers may receive less support and command less respect than foster carers:

> ...the organisational culture that appeared to prevail was that kinship care was not valued in the same way that care provided by in-house foster carers was.

Claire was known to the local authority from the age of five months because of concerns of parental substance misuse and domestic abuse. Sexually abused at the age of six years, she had been placed with her paternal grandmother under s.20 of the Children Act 1989. The girl 'was close to her grandmother: she spent every weekend in her care and had her own bedroom in the house'. No full assessment of the grandmother's capacity to care for her granddaughter or the support she might need had been carried out. The girl exhibited 'emotional distress and her behaviour was difficult to understand...The paternal grandmother often asked CSC [children's social care] for support; she was seen as very demanding'. The girl became too difficult for her grandmother to manage:

> By this time, Claire had been with her paternal grandmother for almost four months, but no formal connected person's assessment had been completed, no therapeutic services or guidance had been provided, and no financial assistance had been given.

SUPPORTING SPECIAL GUARDIANS

A special guardianship order, introduced in the Adoption and Children Act 2002 and used in England and Wales, preserves the legal link between the child and their birth family. When an order is granted, the local authority has no ongoing responsibility as the child is not looked after by the local authority (Simmonds, 2011). The special guardian has parental responsibility for the child's daily care and decisions regarding their upbringing.

Special guardianship was intended to complement adoption and was originally envisaged as a legal option for older children who had a pre-existing relationship with the carer. However, recent research has found that there has been a rise in the use of special guardianship orders for very young children (Harwin *et al*, 2019).

The current study includes six serious case reviews relating to 10 children living with special guardians. Three of the reviews suggest that, once the court had granted the order, children's social care had no further contact.

The case of Shi-Anne, an 18-month-old girl placed with a distant relative on a special guardianship order, discussed earlier, illustrates how the involvement of children's social care ceased with the granting of the order. The girl's mother had a long history of drug misuse and mental illness. A pre-birth assessment had resulted in the unborn child being made subject of a child protection plan. Shi-Anne was a mixed heritage child born with alcohol withdrawal symptoms. Post-birth planning resulted in a foster placement with a twin-track approach for either adoption or special guardianship. The decision was for her to live with a relative who had previously been granted special guardianship for her older sibling:

> It appears that the thought process was that if an SGO was right for her sibling in 2009 [five years earlier], then it must be right for Shi-Anne now, even though the early circumstances of their lives were not similar. Shi-Anne was not being treated as an individual with her own specific needs.

The special guardianship order was granted:

> On 30 January 2015, Shi-Anne went to live with Kandyce Downer and CSC closed the case with the outstanding commitment to three visits before 9 March 2015...There are no records of the support visits ever taking place.

A similar scenario occurred in the case of Bonnie, a two-year-old girl whose mother had been assessed as unable to care for her. Her maternal grandmother was granted a special guardianship order to look after her. The maternal grandfather had a series of unproven allegations of sexual abuse but had not lived in the home for more than 12 years.

The review noted that the case was closed to children's social care six months after the order had been granted: 'Parenting guidance and support would be offered through the Children's Centre and universal services'. Unbeknown to children's social care, soon after the order had been granted, the grandfather returned to live in the same household as the girl and sexually abused her.

Additional orders to provide support

In other cases, the court, when granting a special guardianship order, may make additional orders to support the family. There is an increasing possibility that a supervision order will be made to the local authority to accompany a special guardianship order (Harwin *et al*, 2015): this imposes a duty on the local authority to advise, assist and befriend the child.

A review relating to two young children, both with learning disabilities, serves as an example: 'The Family Court also made an order that the local authority should continue to supervise the children for the following 12 months'. This resulted in substantial support being provided to the family.

The following case is a further example of the court recognising that children with disabilities will need specialist care. The seven-year-old girl had been born with multiple difficulties, including learning disabilities, poor motor skills and damaged kidneys. Her birth mother's mental health was poor and resulted in her daughter having to be fostered at the age of three. A year later, she went to live with her aunt, who was successful in obtaining a special guardianship order. Any difficulties identified during the transition period were attributed to the girl's complex needs and past history, and the social worker provided a positive report to the court:

> The SGO was granted and the Children's Guardian recommended ongoing support because of Child J's complex needs; the court agreed that there would be a family assistance order (FAO) for one year...This named the family support worker (FSW) as the "appropriate officer".

The review noted that a family assistance order has no requirement for a formal plan of how support will be provided. In this case, there were three separate support plans, two had not been implemented and there was a lack of clear purpose, and no reviewing mechanism or contingency arrangements.

SUPPORTING CHILD ARRANGEMENTS ORDERS (FORMERLY RESIDENCE ORDERS)

Child arrangements orders (replacing residence orders in 2014) are made by the court and settle with whom the child will live. Parental responsibility is shared between the carer and the child's parents. When an order is granted, any current care orders are discharged, although the court may attach a supervision order. A child arrangements order allowance may be available in cases where children's social care has previously been involved with the child.

Two Welsh reviews in this study related to a single child subject to a residence order. Two English serious case reviews revealed more complicated circumstances. In one, the foster family household contained three older siblings on residence orders, plus two foster children subject to care orders. The other case related to a single woman whose household contained two children she had adopted, and three for whom a residence order had been granted.

In all instances where a residence order had been granted, the children had originally been fostered with the family. In most cases, the birth mother had initially made an informal arrangement with the carer to look after her child. Child D provides an example of the importance of practitioners fully understanding the legal status of the child. Shortly after his birth, Child D was given to a neighbour to be brought up by her in a private fostering arrangement:

> Child D was fostered privately by his carer for over nine years before a residence order was made. When XXX Social Services Department became aware of the arrangement, some steps towards carrying out the statutory duties were taken but written reports required after each visit were not completed and there was little detail on the file...There was uncertainty and confusion among professional staff over the status of Child D throughout his life which no agency sought to clarify and resolve.

Child D had a history of challenging behaviour but no enquiry had been made into the underlying causes. When he was almost 17 years old, his foster carer found him dead in his bedroom.

The review identified how uncertainty with regard to a child's legal status could impact on the child's welfare and safety. When households contain a number of children living under different types of arrangement, clarity about practitioners' roles and responsibilities in relation to individual children will be essential to ensuring their well-being and safety.

SUPPORTING ADOPTERS

A placement order is an order made by the court authorising a local authority to place a child for adoption with any prospective adopters who may be chosen by the authority.

(Adoption and Children Act 2002, s.21(1))

A placement order continues until an adoption order is granted. When a local authority places a child for adoption, the placement is subject to regular review.

When the child has been placed for adoption, the first review must be held no more than four weeks after placement, the second no more than three months after this and subsequent reviews held at six-monthly intervals until an adoption order is made, or the child is no longer placed with the prospective adopter.

(DfE, 2013a, p.103, para 5.35)

The review must consider a range of issues, including the child's needs, welfare and development, and whether any changes need to be made to meet the child's needs or assist their development.

The adoption agency must also review the approval of prospective adopters 'whenever the adoption agency considers it necessary but otherwise not more than one year after approval and thereafter at intervals of not more than one year' (HM Government, 2013, 30D). The findings from the review will inform the decision of whether or not the prospective adopter continues to be suitable to adopt a child.

Once an adoption order is made, the adopters have parental responsibility and the local authority has no further legislative oversight. An adoption allowance can be paid to eligible adopters before and after the adoption order is granted, under the Adoption Support Services (Local Authorities) Regulations 2005 in England; the Adoption Support Services and Allowances (Scotland) Regulations 2009; and the Adoption Support Services (Wales) Regulations 2005. As this is means-tested, it is subject to annual review, providing an opportunity for some degree of oversight. The local authority is also responsible for assessing an adoptive family's need for ongoing support. Since 2015, the Adoption Support Fund (ASF) has become available to adopters (and subsequently special guardians) in England, and provides financial support for a range of therapeutic services. However, research by Adoption UK (2019) found that 70 per cent of adopters struggle to get the help and support that their child needs.

The serious case reviews included in the present study suggest that when concerns about a prospective adoptive placement arise, they may not result in an assessment to decide whether additional support is needed or if the placement meets the child's needs.

The following case illustrates how, despite a number of concerns arising while a placement order existed, the court went on to grant an adoption order. The child had become looked after at birth and initially lived with foster carers for nearly a year. A care order and placement order were granted and the child was placed with a prospective adoptive family. The child remained as a looked after child until the adoption order was granted eight months later. During this time, the child suffered a number of bruises and injuries that were routinely brought to the attention of the medical profession:

> All the evidence from the medical professionals indicated that the injuries the child sustained between November and March were accidental. No safeguarding concerns were raised.

Although this information had been shared with children's social care, the record showed that 'The professionals and the review record make no reference to the child having a bruise'. Once the adoption order had been granted, an adoption support plan was in place although the parents 'did not identify any ongoing support needs over and above those needed by any child'. Sadly, within the month of the adoption order having been granted, the child suffered injuries at home and died in intensive care.

A review relating to three children placed together with prospective adopters again highlights how initial concerns, having been identified prior to the application to adopt being submitted to the court, had not been acknowledged. The prospective adoptive mother had reported difficulties in her relationship with one of the siblings: 'M complained about the lack of support and requested more help, stating that they would not submit the adoption application to court until the situation with Child C improved'. In addition, the health visitor 'became aware of, but did not share information about two injuries which might have been sustained accidentally'. The prospective adopters submitted their application to adopt, and a scheduled statutory review was cancelled: 'There had been no re-evaluation of whether the placement was viable and still in the children's best interests'.

The adopters had not asked for post-adoption support, and the review found no record of further social work visits. It was some eight years later, as a result of another sibling making a series of allegations of physical abuse against his adopters, that the police and children's social care had become involved.

PROFESSIONALS' LOYALTY TO CARERS

The role of the supervising social worker, also known as a fostering social worker, encompasses both the support and supervisory aspects of work undertaken with foster carers (Brown *et al*, 2014). It is essential that, when visiting foster placements, supervising social workers' assessments are objective.

In a number of the reviews, it became clear that impartiality had been threatened. This may occur when the social worker who assessed the foster carer continues to supervise them once approved. A sense of loyalty to "their foster carer" may cloud future assessments and judgements. This dual role was a feature noted in an historical case of sexual abuse and resulted in the social worker being unable to acknowledge the possibility of child abuse:

> *The local authority management review identified 'an organisational culture within which individual supervising social workers felt pride when "their" foster carers did well'. The reverse of this may be a natural defensiveness when foster carers are criticised.*

A lack of objectivity may also occur when local authorities have worked with foster carers over a long period. This can result in established mindsets and "group think" that are difficult to change, a feature acknowledged in the following review:

> *Paradoxically, the depth of knowledge of the F family and their fostering style that was built up through the extraordinary continuity of contact between the foster carers and their SSWs [supervising social workers] may have hindered rather than helped an objective assessment of the strengths and weaknesses of the foster home.*

In another historical case of sexual abuse, the carers had fostered for 17 years. Allegations of abuse were not seen as credible and the male foster carer's history of offending, anger and aggression discounted:

> *...from the beginning, the fostering service valued them highly because of the flexibility and willingness to offer a range of placement.*

The tendency to view incidents through an overly optimistic lens was evident in other types of placement. A review relating to two young children with learning disabilities living with distant relatives under a special guardianship order serves as an example:

> *Overall the desire for the placement to be successful, especially for staff with a continuing relationship with the children, may have obscured their judgement.*

In other cases, the social workers' role may be compromised when foster carers are able to weight the relationship in their favour. The reviews showed that this may occur when carers (in the following case, adopters) are articulate and well educated:

> *The parents presented as a well-educated and articulate couple who had been able to access resources and support previously. They were very well regarded by each of the agencies as good parents who had already successfully adopted…Given how strongly this view was held, the injuries that the child sustained were never considered as anything other than childhood accidents.*

Alternatively, a review relating to a child with a range of complex disabilities highlighted how false assumptions about carers could affect assessments and decision-making:

> *Decisions in this case were made based on presumptions. There was a presumption that the foster mother was an expert in children with complex disabilities and should be deferred to.*

The balance of power between professionals and carers was an issue acknowledged by Narey and Owers (2018), who 'reject the notion that foster carers should be defined as professionals with equivalent status – for example – to social workers' (p.11). They argue that social workers need to retain a sense of respectful uncertainty.

ISSUES RELATED TO CHILDREN'S ASSESSMENTS AND REVIEWS

When an adoption order, child arrangements order or special guardianship order is granted, the involvement of the local authority generally ends. In contrast, the health, well-being and safety of looked after children are the responsibility of the state. To ensure that they are safeguarded and thrive in foster care or when placed for adoption, children are subject to statutory review. Reviews are carried out within 20 working days of the child becoming looked after, three months after the initial review, and subsequently every six months.

The role of the Independent Reviewing Officer

The National Association of Independent Reviewing Officers (2016) has produced an IRO toolkit that includes a code of practice. Mr Justice Jackson noted that 'the core task of an IRO is to manage the review and to chair that review in a way which should:'

- *Hold the welfare of the child as the paramount consideration;*
- *Ensure the voice of the child is heard clearly in the process;*

- *Subject the local authority care plan to critical scrutiny and challenge the local authority in relation to that care plan if necessary.*

(England and Wales High Court (Family Division) Decisions, 2012, para 197)

It is the responsibility of the Independent Reviewing Officer (IRO) to chair Looked After Children (LAC) reviews, monitor the appropriateness of the care plan and its implementation, and decide whether it is being achieved in a timely manner. In preparation for review meetings, the IRO must speak with the child and social worker and be provided with or have access to relevant reports, plans and background information. The IRO is also responsible for ensuring that those attending the meeting make a meaningful contribution in order to inform the decision-making about what actions are needed to advance the child's care plan (Department for Children, Schools and Families (DCSF), 2010).

Reviews for looked after children differ from those for children placed for adoption. The major difference is that once the child has been placed with the prospective adopters, they 'will always have a major role and must be consulted, whereas the extent to which birth parents are consulted and involved will be a matter for the agency's discretion depending on the circumstances of the case' (DfE, 2013a, p.103, para 5.37).

When children are placed for adoption, the reviews, prior to the adoption order being granted, may be referred to as adoption reviews. This terminology was used in one of the Welsh child practice reviews for an adopted child:

> *The second adoption review was attended by the child's social worker and the adoption social worker and chaired by the Independent Reviewing Officer.*

The template for recording the "adoption reviews" was seen as not enabling robust scrutiny:

> *The adoption review template did not promote the IRO to capture a full picture of the significant events in the child's life since being placed with the parents. A holistic understanding of the child's story was not gained.*

Other issues can also hamper the role of the IRO. The National Children's Bureau's national survey (2016) suggested that excessive caseloads may be having a negative impact. The study identified that, outside of London, caseloads held by IROs were well above the recommended limit (Jelicic *et al*, 2013). In a court ruling, the excessive case load held by the IRO was one of the number of issues highlighted as an obstacle that had impacted on his ability to ensure children's safety:

- *A caseload of more than three times the good practice guidance at times;*

- *Inadequate training in general and legal principles;*

- *The absence of access to legal advice;*

- *Inadequate supervision and monitoring or appraisal by managers;*

- *Missing social work reports in advance of the review from time to time;*

- *A tick-box system, driven by mandatory performance indicators, creating the illusion of action without any evidence of the quality of the achievement.*

(England and Wales High Court (Family Division) Decisions (2012, para 137))

Identified inadequacies in LAC reviews

A crucial moment for information to be shared is at the reviews for looked after children. These are the forums used to ensure that plans are appropriate to safeguard and promote the welfare of the child and to monitor the progress of the child's care plan. Their success depends on having access to all relevant information concerning the child and their circumstances. To accomplish this, relevant professionals should be invited to attend or submit a written report to the IRO.

A number of the serious case reviews revealed that this did not always happen, and decisions were based on incomplete information. For example, a review of a case concerning two siblings shows how things can go wrong. The children were of dual heritage and subjects of final care orders on the grounds of neglect. They had been placed with foster carers who had physically abused them on a regular basis. Education and health staff had rarely, if ever, attended review meetings:

> *In this case, there is no evidence that school staff were invited to attend any of the reviews or to provide a report or verbal comments. On no occasion was a Personal Education Plan available to the review. In addition, the school nurse attended one review, but there is no evidence that she was invited to or attended any of the others.*

Similar issues arose in the case of an eight-year-old girl. Although health needs had been identified and the school had been closely involved, 'none of these professionals or agencies were represented at this important meeting'.

The review relating to this girl also brought to light the impact on practice of the considerable work pressures felt by front-line services in meeting the demands of their safeguarding role. This resulted in a pragmatic approach to reduce workloads and rationalise finite resources, based on the commonly-held assumption that children in the care of the local authority are safe. It was argued that, in principle, LAC reviews, chaired by an IRO, would be the forum for 'risk management and safety planning'. The conclusions reached by the serious case review were rather different:

> ...in practice LAC reviews are not a substitute for child protection case conferences: the focus of these meetings is not on protection; it is on care planning. Risk and safeguarding issues are not routinely discussed and the full multi-agency group is not included, as evidenced in this case.

The serious case reviews also identified that on occasions LAC reviews overly relied on the information given by the foster carers. In the case of the 10-year-old girl, sexually abused by the adopted son of the carer, the LAC review had made little reference to changes in household membership. Information from the police and youth offending team had not been accessed:

> The report comments that the case illustrates that a local authority cannot rely on a foster carer to inform them of events occurring in the lives of those living in, staying frequently or routinely visiting the foster home.

When IROs do not fulfil their role or fail to robustly pursue missing records, a review cannot accomplish its purpose. The following case, relating to a baby going through the adoption process, highlights how the regularity of reviews is not enough if the IRO does not carry out quality assurance and challenge decisions:

> The lack of a core assessment as a task of the first review was not followed up or its absence challenged; the lack of an Initial Health Assessment was noted, but its lack also not challenged. The records of the review did not clearly focus on tasks or the role of the professionals present and no clear goals were set.

Valuing LAC reviews and the IRO

The findings from the current study suggest that practitioners and agencies did not always value LAC reviews or the role of the IRO. This reflects the findings from the National Children's Bureau's national survey, which found 'some IROs do not feel the service is valued or taken seriously' (Jelicic *et al*, 2013, p.14). The review relating to the eight-year-old girl, mentioned earlier, highlighted this issue:

> Discussions with the case group about the purpose of LAC reviews in the life of a looked after child revealed a general sense of lethargy about these meetings. There seemed to be no investment in these reviews as a process that improved outcomes for children. They were felt to be just 'an added thing that needed to be done'; to be ticked off in a long list of process requirements that hampered rather than helped the busy life of a front line social work team.

When IROs have concerns about an individual case, these are generally resolved through informal ways. However, in situations where a dispute resolution protocol is used, the National Children's Bureau's survey showed that one-third of IROs were not satisfied that their concerns had been addressed (Jelicic *et al*, 2013).

A review of a case relating to a 12-year-old boy illustrates how the role and function of the IRO may not be understood and how, consequently, concerns can remain unaddressed. The same IRO chaired all the many LAC reviews that the boy had been involved in. The IRO had frequently met with the child and the records show how they had attempted to ensure that the boy was listened to and his voice heard. Unfortunately, the concerns raised had not always been addressed, and resulted in the instigation of the Dispute Resolution process; the response of the Acting Director to this was not in accordance with procedures:

> *The Review Team was of the view that if senior leaders within Children Services do not utilise the expertise and knowledge of IROs and do not respond to their concerns about practice and decision-making, then this leaves looked after children even more vulnerable.*

In other cases, the recommendations made by the IRO were dismissed. For example, a core assessment had been recommended by the IRO in a case relating to a six-year-old girl and her older brother, but had not been completed. The social worker and manager thought it not necessary because they had information from the assessments and reviews for the other four siblings who had come into care. This decision had not been shared with the IRO.

In contrast, difficulties may arise when the IRO does not take the lead and resolve differences between professionals. The findings from the following review illustrate this:

> *The statutory Looked After Children reviews for Child "S" were well attended by professionals, differences between them were addressed but not resolved. This case needed one of the professionals to take control and ensure differences were resolved. It was within the remit of the Independent Reviewing Officer to do this.*

The child's perspective

There is a presumption that the child will attend and contribute to the LAC review. However, even the best efforts of the IRO may fail to ensure that the child's voice is heard and informs the decisions taken at the LAC review:

> *Despite PB's numerous placements, there was very little analysis in LAC meetings about PB's placement breakdowns and whilst the precipitating incident was often clear, there was little evidence of PB's views as to what had happened, despite the contacts made by the IRO.*

This review went on to question whether the existing systems for LAC reviews may alienate young people and inadvertently lead them to feel stigmatised by the process.

The suicide of Child A, a 17-year-old boy with ADHD, illustrates how not attending to what children are saying can have tragic outcomes. The boy had voiced his fear of leaving care, and how unprepared he felt, to all the professionals with whom he had contact. The report identified:

> ...that all the agencies outside of the local authority looked to each other to find the answers...compounded by the missed opportunity that the IRO service had to ensure challenge and scrutiny where there was evidence of poor quality care planning and to escalate concerns to a senior level.

Children value practitioners who listen to them. In this case, to gain greater understanding of children's perceptions of IROs, the reviewers had sought the views of a group of young people who had recently left or were in the process of leaving care:

> They all agreed that the role of the IRO was very important to them. They had various experiences of their IRO and the most dominant reflection was around the fact that when everyone changed for one reason or another (change of social worker, school or placement) the IRO was the most consistent person. They all spoke of experiences when their IRO held others to account and at times stopped them spinning.

To ensure the participation and involvement of a disabled child in the review process, additional factors must be addressed. It may require the IRO to draw on extra resources and time to ensure that the child's voice is heard (DCSF, 2009).

The serious case reviews included in this study highlight a number of barriers that can impede IROs in successfully carrying out their responsibilities. Despite the shortcomings that occur in some cases, the reviews suggest that it is a service highly valued by children. The fostering review by Narey and Owens (2018) supports this finding:

> ...we feel IROs play a crucial role in ensuring children's views are recognised, supported and sustained. We would like to see IROs becoming independent of local authorities and having more authority, in order to be fully independent and effective, and to be able to ensure decisions are in the best interests of the child.

(Narey and Owens, 2018)

This perception of the role of IROs mirrors that expressed to the Children's Minister in a collective letter from 'associations and individual academics who worked together to defend the rights of children and families during the passage of the Children and Social Work Act 2017' (BECOME, 2018).

ASSESSMENTS AND REVIEWS OF FOSTER CARERS

Approval of all foster carers must be reviewed, and a decision about suitability made, within a year of approval, and thereafter whenever it is felt necessary, but at intervals of no more than twelve months. The review must consider whether the foster carer and their household continue to be suitable.

(DfE, 2013b, p.18)

Research findings emphasise the importance of continuous monitoring and review of foster carers and the value of carefully recording past allegations and concerns about carers (Biehal *et al*, 2014).

The review should place any new allegation in historical context, include checks in relation to any new members of the household, and take account of the views of the foster carers, the children placed there, other children and adults in the foster home, and the social worker responsible for the children.

The guidance and regulations relating to reviews of foster homes had not always been adhered to, as observed in some of the serious case reviews. The case of a couple, where the male carer had sexually abused three girls whom they were fostering, provides an example. The case review noted that initially the husband had been the main carer while his wife continued to work. Ill health meant that she had to give up work and become a full-time carer. Both carers developed significant health problems, and the male carer also had an alcohol problem:

Despite these changes their ability to provide appropriate care was not re-assessed ...Although fostering reviews took place, they did not happen annually, as required by regulations, and it is not clear what information was presented to the fostering panel following each review.

The carrying out of a review of foster carers does not guarantee that the information is analysed and issues addressed. The following case of a two-year-old boy, who tragically died three months after having been placed with an experienced foster mother, serves as an example:

It does appear that the annual reviews took place on time, but there is little evidence of concerns being considered in a cohesive way, thus there was a lack of opportunity to put together the sequence of events and concerns, which with hindsight, can be seen to be accumulations.

A learning point from this case review was the need for regular and consistent supervision of foster placements, especially for nonverbal and pre-school children.

Other cases highlighted the difficulties that can arise when annual reviews of foster carers assume a "competency approach". Such an approach discourages any exploration of concerns or challenges of the accuracy of the information. A serious case review in relation to the sexual abuse of eight primary school-aged children by a male foster carer is an example. The couple had 30 children placed with them over a five-year period:

> *The fostering support worker told the SCR [serious case review] that her work with the foster carers in the build up to reviews was to encourage them to gather and present information, which demonstrated their skill and knowledge in relation to each of the competencies. Where there was a shortfall, further information could be obtained or opportunities and mechanisms for improvement identified. This approach encouraged the gathering of positive evidence and did not encourage the review to discuss or explore concerns.*

SUMMARY OF KEY FINDINGS

- The support available to carers depends on the legal status of the child. Support for foster carers is the most comprehensive due to the underpinning legal framework and because carers are part of a "team around the child". Although the majority of serious case reviews showed that regular visits and support had been provided to foster carers, this was not always the case. Many reviews noted how organisational disruption and staffing levels within children's social care affected the level of support that foster carers received.

- When a number of different agencies are involved with the child, the care plan should provide clarity about which ones are responsible for providing the different aspects of support to carers and the child.

- A fostering allowance and additional financial support are available to foster carers. Any concerns that a carer's primary motivation for looking after a child is financial must be thoroughly investigated. A failure to do so may place the child at risk of neglect or harm.

- When children are living away from their parents in a private fostering arrangement, the parent or carer is responsible for notifying the local authority. Information about how this is to be done must be widely available in a range of languages to ensure that this is understood. Visits are required and must be undertaken by the local authority at the stipulated intervals.

- Children may live with family and friends, also known as kinship care or connected persons care. This can be an informal arrangement or a placement made by the local authority. When a child is placed within the family, relative carers should receive the same support and supervision as other foster carers. There is, however, a widely held assumption that family members have a moral obligation to provide care and subsequently may not be given the same degree of support. In families with a history of chaotic living, placing a child with wider kin may not provide the hoped-for safe environment.

● The granting of a special guardianship order usually results in the case being closed by children's social care. In some cases, a time-limited supervision order or family assistance order may accompany the special guardianship order. A supervision order ensures that additional help and oversight are given to the placement. A family assistance order can provide additional support, but there is no requirement for a formal plan. Given that the children who were the subject of serious case reviews frequently did not have a prior relationship with their special guardian, the question must be asked whether the equivalent of the adoption support plan should be offered to special guardians.

● In cases where an adoption order has been granted, the local authority has no legislative oversight. However, concerns that arise while a placement order is active must be acknowledged and fully evaluated prior to the application to adopt being submitted to the court. Once the adoption order is granted, new parents may be eligible for an adoption allowance and should be offered an adoption support plan. If an adoption allowance is granted, the annual review may provide an opportunity for a degree of oversight. In England, they may also obtain support through the Adoption Support Fund (ASF). However, such support is discretionary and depends on the funding being agreed and the adopters accepting it.

● The Children Act 1989 (Part 111) places a duty on local authorities 'to safeguard and promote the welfare of children within their area who are in need'. Children who have been adopted or who live with special guardians may be "children in need" as defined by the Act. Indeed, the reviews showed that many of these children qualified as "children in need" and would therefore have been eligible for services.

● Where carers are well known to professionals and agencies, it can result in a loss of objectivity. A sense of loyalty to "their carers" may threaten impartiality, result in over-optimism and undermine the ability to safeguard children. Reflective supervision and professional challenge are effective ways to think about and reassess professional roles and boundaries.

● In some cases, the balance of power between professionals and carers can become skewed and an inappropriate amount of power comes to rest with the carers. This may be exacerbated by a reluctance to challenge articulate and well-educated carers, or due to concerns of being seen as discriminatory when carers are of a different sexual orientation or from a different cultural background to that of the professional. When this occurs, social workers need to retain a sense of respectful uncertainty and raise any concerns with their supervisor.

● Looked After Children (LAC) reviews and the role of the IRO are not always sufficiently valued. Local authorities and senior managers should ensure that the IRO's role and function are understood and utilised effectively. A result of such a failure is that LAC reviews are not informed by the wishes and views of the child. Where children consistently express strongly held views, these must be recorded and taken into account during the LAC review and should not be ignored or over-ruled. The serious case reviews point to the pivotal role of the IRO, which, the evidence suggests, may need to be strengthened.

- The pressures on front-line practitioners and the assumption that, by the very fact of coming into care, looked after children are protected from harm can result in information held by agencies, such as health, education and the police, not being included in LAC reviews. The review meeting can only be effective if all the relevant practitioners either attend the meeting or submit a written report. In many cases, this did not occur. A robust and multi-agency approach is needed.

- The reviews of foster carers do not always comply with guidance and regulations. Difficulties can arise when a "competency approach" is taken. The information provided by foster carers should be checked and analysed and any concerns fully explored.

Chapter 6
Smoke and mirrors

Something that is described as smoke and mirrors is intended to make you believe that something is being done or is true, when it is not.

(McIntosh, 2013)

THE ASSUMPTION OF SAFETY

In the majority of cases, children living with foster carers, adopters or special guardians are safe from serious harm. For example, there were 56,160 children living with foster families on 31 March 2019 in England (The Fostering Network, 2019). In contrast, only 39 serious case reviews related to children living with foster carers at the time of their death or serious harm, during the 12 years covered by the current study.

Allegations of abuse and neglect, however, are more frequent. The work by Nina Biehal and colleagues (2014) for the NSPCC found four allegations per 100 children in foster care across the UK each year for the period under study. Data for adoption and special guardianship were not available. Viewed over a carer's fostering career, a more recent survey suggests that one-third of 4,037 responding foster carers reported experiencing one or more allegation of abuse or neglect (Lawson and Cann, 2019). The impact of an allegation is inevitably profound:

> *It is obviously a distressing time for the foster carers. They are too often left not knowing timescales, not being given access to independent support, and having financial support removed.*

(Lawson and Cann, 2019, p.31)

An allegation does not necessarily mean that children have been harmed. Nina Biehal and colleagues (2014) found that only 26 per cent of allegations were confirmed: 'This represents less than one substantiated allegation per 100 children in foster care across the UK each year' (Biehal *et al*, 2014, p.11). However, unsubstantiated allegations do not mean that children are safe. Their study reported that only 30 per cent of allegations were considered unfounded; 43 per cent remained unsubstantiated due to a lack of evidence. The finding suggests that the numbers of children abused and neglected in foster care could be considerably higher (Biehal *et al*, 2014).

The small proportion of serious incidents of abuse and neglect involving children living in foster care may result in professionals holding overly optimistic views of foster care, adoption and special guardianship. Such placements are perceived as places of refuge and nurture for children, many of whom have a history of abuse and neglect, as one review in this study noted:

> *There was an assumption by professionals that as "F" was a Child in Care, he was safe. The fostering panel did not provide effective challenge to "F's" foster carers, allowing their actions to often go without scrutiny.*

To offer a home to a child who has had an abusive start in life is seen as a worthy deed, particularly because the experience of harmful parenting will have affected children's thinking, behaviour and development. The general public and professionals alike tend to perceive the offer of a home to an abused and neglected child as a courageous act. Carers and adopters are seen as heroes undertaking difficult tasks and deserving all the support they can get. This assumption is stronger in relation to caring for children with disabilities.

Sadly, the current study of serious case reviews shows that such assumptions are not always reliable. Although the cases where children have died or suffered significant harm are a tiny proportion of all children fostered, adopted or living with special guardians, nonetheless they must not be ignored:

> *The assumption cannot be made that because a child is looked after by the local authority that they are safe or that their needs are fully met.*

(Independent Inquiry into Child Sexual Abuse, 2019)

The challenge facing professionals is both to meet the carers' needs for support and ensure that children are protected and their developmental needs are met.

NOT ALL CARERS ARE HEROES

To accept the care of disabled children enhances the perception of carers as heroes and is personified by the following serious case review. Siblings A and B, both with a degree of learning disability, had been removed from their parents at an early age due to abuse and neglect. They had been placed with relative carers who had three teenage birth children. Both children subsequently suffered 10 years of abuse, neglect and cruelty at the carers' hands. The review noted that practitioners had accepted the relative carers' projection of themselves as "heroic carers" who were dealing with very difficult disabled children. It was through this lens that various bruises and allegations of abuse were seen:

> This perception of the disability being the key issue became an influencing factor in the effective safeguarding of the siblings, where evidence of possible physical abuse was described by the relative carer as difficulties in managing children with complex needs and behaviours.

For these and other children, their placement was neither a place of refuge and nurture, nor were their carers heroes. The review relating to Claire, an eight-year-old girl, serves as a further example of a failure to reflect on established perceptions. The birth family had been known to children's social care because of concerns relating to domestic abuse and parental drug and alcohol misuse. Claire's name had been placed on the Child Protection Register. At the age of six, she had been sexually abused by a friend of her mother's. She became a looked after child and went to live with her paternal grandmother. This did not last more than two months, after which time she was placed with foster carers. Sadly, this placement offered no protection; the sexual abuse was renewed at the hands of the male foster carer. The review team in this case spoke about the difficulties in "thinking the unthinkable".

A review relating to the case of a teenage boy summarises this issue well:

> The recognition that foster carers may not be all they appear to be, or that a child may be at risk in a foster placement is entirely dependent on the professionals' inherent willingness to entertain the possibility that such things do happen.

The significance of being able to "think the unthinkable" was highlighted in a number of reviews in this study and identified in an investigative report by the Independent Inquiry into Child Sexual Abuse (2019). An historical case involving the sexual abuse of numerous children at the hands of their foster carer highlights this and the possible consequences for the children's safety. Teachers and social workers had noted that one of the children 'showed a very high level of sexualised behaviour' but no professional had suggested that abuse by the foster carer might explain his behaviour. The review reported that this may have been the result of:

> ...an underlying assumption among professionals that this child was not being abused in her foster home because she and others placed there were safe, either because they were in public care or more specifically because they were in foster care.

The review identified two lessons to be learned: first, the importance of organisations enabling staff to consider alternative, unpalatable explanations about children's problems; and second, to help staff acknowledge that, although unusual, a child might be abused by a professional carer.

Specific issues could also influence practitioners' perspectives of carers. An inquiry relating to two gay male foster carers who had sexually abused a number of boys concluded that the sexual orientation of the carers 'was a significant cause of people not thinking the unthinkable... It was clear that a number of staff were afraid of being thought homophobic'.

CONTROLLING EXTERNAL SCRUTINY

Not all the reviews in the present study provided detailed information of the course of events leading up to the incident. Where information was available, there is considerable evidence that carers who had abused children in their care had attempted to control both the degree of oversight they received and their relationship with professionals.

Removing children from school

Adopted children are more likely than children in the general population to be excluded from school (Adoption UK, 2017). Fifteen per cent of adopted children had at least one fixed period of exclusion, compared with 11.8 per cent of looked after children and 2.3 per cent of all children (Timpson Review of School Exclusion, 2019).

In two of the seven reviews relating to adopted children, a striking phenomenon was adopters who had actively sought to control all contact with the external world. In both cases, the serious case reviews suggested that this was exemplified by the use of elective home education to avoid any scrutiny of the adopters' care of the children; outsiders were unwelcome.

One review related to five children, initially privately fostered, who had been subsequently adopted or placed with the carer under a residence order. The case illustrates how concerns over the welfare of one child had resulted in their carer withdrawing the two children of school age from mainstream education:

> Mrs Spry removed Belinda from school, removing an important source of monitoring of Belinda's welfare. Mrs Spry had removed Anne from school just over a year earlier.

In the second review, relating to another adoptive family, the children had never entered the education system. The mother, of three children adopted from abroad, championed home education and was well known in home education circles. However, the report noted:

> ...that M [the adoptive mother] was an unsuitable person to provide it; and the nature of the isolated environment in which the children were educated by M enhanced her capacity to subject them to abuse without

the risk of observation, so minimising the opportunity for disclosure by the children.

The report highlighted the abuse suffered by these children and the adoptive mother's control over them:

As early as age 13, until A gave birth at age 17, M's scheme to monitor A's ovulation and facilitate repeated attempts to ensure A conceived and carried a child to term via artificial insemination caused A profound emotional difficulties which will have inevitably disrupted her capacity for education. M then ensured that A and B lied to various health care professionals about the true circumstances of the pregnancy.

The local authority education department only became aware of the children following a child protection referral to children's social care; the two younger children were then aged 11 and 12 years.

Similar to the two adoption cases, not being registered at a school was an issue in the tragic life of a privately fostered boy. Shortly after his birth, the boy's parents had given him to a neighbour to be brought up in a private fostering arrangement, later resulting in a residence order being granted. When the boy was aged 11 years, the family moved to a different local authority and from this age the boy 'was not registered to attend any school, nor was he registered with any GP'. He became invisible to education, health and children's services. However, the police knew him well. Between the ages of 12 and 17 years, he had been arrested on 24 occasions for incidents including assault, criminal damage and theft. He had been found drunk from a young age and 'spoke to officers repeatedly about and demonstrated attempts to self harm'. He died in his bedroom at the age of 17, 'due to contracting bronchopneumonia, and taking a number of drugs which, when combined, had potentially fatal levels of morphine'.

The challenge facing professionals is to identify concerns about children's welfare and safety when they are removed from the general oversight that school attendance provides. The most recent Government guidance, *Elective Home Education*, acknowledges 'the increasing concern that some children educated at home may not be in safe environments' (DfE, 2019b, p.4). Although local authorities have the same safeguarding responsibilities for children educated at home as for other children, when children are hidden or become anonymous, it becomes difficult to fulfil this role.

In law, the responsibility for a child's education rests with their parents. It is their right to choose to educate their child at home rather than at school and there is no legislation that deals specifically with home education. Moreover, 'there are no specific legal requirements as to the content of home education, provided the parents meet their duty in s.7 of the Education Act 1996' (DfE, 2019b, para 2.4).

The Virtual School Head (VSH)

The appointment of a Virtual School Head (VSH) has become a statutory requirement for local authorities (Children and Families Act 2014; DfE, 2018b). Their role is to give extra impetus to the local authorities' duty to promote the education of looked after children and those who have previously been looked after, including children adopted from care and those subject to a special guardianship order.

All the children included in the case reviews, who were either home educated or absent from school for long periods, had been adopted or subject to a residence order. It is not surprising that none of the reviews made reference to a VSH, because in every case either the adopted children were not known to children's social care at the time they had been removed from school, or school removal had taken place prior to the introduction of VSHs.

Failing to take children to medical appointments

A further way in which carers sought to control outside scrutiny was to avoid bringing children to pre-arranged appointments. For example, the foster carer responsible for the care of two siblings spoke to her health visitor 'regarding Child F's serious bedwetting problem'. The children's GP re-referred the boy to an enuresis clinic, but he was never taken. The review noted that 'No one seemed to note the significance of a foster carer failing to bring a child to appointments relating to his health needs'.

Similar issues were identified in the case of a baby who had died in foster care from non-accidental injuries. It had been reported that the foster carer had a history of not taking children in her care to medical appointments. When the baby was placed in her care, the health visitor had been concerned about the baby's continuing weight loss and 'on the last visit she advised Mrs A to take Child V to the GP regarding her weight loss but this was not done'. The baby spent 51 days with her foster carers before being taken by ambulance to the Accident and Emergency Department where she then died. 'She had a total of 13 rib fractures which were thought to have occurred four weeks before death, with evidence of a recent rib-fracture to one rib'.

Apparent co-operation

There were various examples in the reviews where carers had sought to control professionals' scrutiny through misleading them or by dividing professional opinion.

The following case illustrates how foster carers sought to deflect professional scrutiny by apparent co-operation. PB, a 12-year-old boy, had come into care because his parents were unable to manage his behaviour. He was placed with a single male foster carer. This placement ended due to the carer's ill health. The boy had then been placed in an educational residential setting during the week and weekends, and holidays were spent with another single male foster carer. Professionals viewed both single male carers positively.

The boy soon started going missing from school and was often found at his second carer's home. Concerns were raised about the gifts given to him by this carer and the carer's failure to routinely report the boy's unscheduled presence in his home. It transpired that both his foster carers had sexually abused this boy. The review noted:

> There is evidence in records, which suggests that both foster carers misled workers whilst appearing to work in partnership and stressing how much they were doing for the young people in their care – arguably, a form of disguised compliance, which can be used to keep professionals at a distance.

CONTROLLING THE NARRATIVE – INFLUENCING PROFESSIONAL PERSPECTIVES

Carers who abuse children use a number of "manipulative styles" to control professionals' oversight and understanding of what is happening to the children in their care (Sullivan and Quayle, 2012).

Creating a positive impression

In several of the reviews, it was clear that carers had sought to control professionals' opinions and views about them and the childcare they were providing. This could be done by creating a positive impression on professionals and so balancing the power of the relationship in their favour. Carers presented themselves as very flexible to practitioners' requests and displayed an apparent focus on the needs of the children for whom they were caring. An historical review of foster carers who had sexually abused numerous children over a 20-year period illustrates this phenomenon:

> They would accept placements of children with a range of needs and were co-operative when children had to be placed quickly. They were perceived as having worked in a very open way with birth parents... the foster carers took trouble to provide photos and mementos for the parents of the children who were placed with them and for "life story work" to help children who were moving into permanent family homes.

Carers' presentation of being positive and proactive may lull practitioners into a false sense of security. It is important to focus not just on the foster carers' behaviours but, more importantly, on the responses of each and every child for whom they care.

Avoiding oversight

Another method that carers may use to shield themselves from professional scrutiny was to avoid direct professional contact and routine oversight. This was a feature in many reviews involving foster families. In seven reviews, it was noted that foster carers were reluctant to take up training opportunities or to participate in foster care support networks.

Two historical cases of sexual abuse provide examples. One review involved the sexual abuse of some eight primary school aged children by their male carer, who had sought to restrict professional oversight by not attending support groups or training sessions. Another related to a fostering household where the male carer had physically and sexually abused five children in his care. An interview with the female carer for the serious case review 'described how although she feels Mr F wanted to foster with the best intentions, he assumed control from the beginning by refusing to attend all the specified training'.

Unsettling behaviour

Carers could also control the narrative by intimidating or disquieting behaviour directed at both birth parents and professionals.

The inquiry report, included in this study, illustrates how abusive male foster carers had sought to control the narrative by grooming the parents of children for whom they provided respite care. To do this, they had used tactics such as undermining the parent's confidence, and getting the parent to side with them against children's social care. One single parent, whose twins went for respite care to these carers, reported how they had been initially charming and helpful towards her and she had believed that her children were well cared for. However, as time went on, her opinion changed; she reported that they were:

> ...ignorant and rude and had the impression that professionals would not have got very far with challenging him as she felt that CF and IW had a sense of themselves as powerful, that everything had to be on their terms, and "they thought they were more authority than anybody".

These foster carers had also successfully intimidated their social worker:

> There was evidence that as FSW2 tried to work with the carers to discuss issues of concern to her, the response from the carers was aggressive and dismissive...She described the visits...where CF, IW and the neighbour (who herself had issues with social services) would subject her to a "barrage" of complaints and issues.

She reported that she felt bullied and intimidated by them.

A further example of controlling the narrative through hostile behaviour is found in the review relating to Mr F:

> During this time there is clear evidence that social workers were concerned about the behaviour of Mr and Mrs F towards staff, but continued to fail to challenge this adequately and consider the implications for the children living within the household.

Abusive carers could also be "intimidating". In another case of sexual abuse, the practitioners who had met with the male carer in the home environment reported that he was 'arrogant and controlling, self-evidently the more powerful adult in the marriage and dictatorial in his attitude to the children'. However, he had been successful in dividing professional opinion. The fostering support worker 'found him occasionally difficult but never offensive or angry with her or in review meetings with social workers'.

The review summed up the man's efforts to control the professionals' perception of him by presenting different personae:

> However, to have adopted an aggressive, insidious or overt controlling approach in his dealings with all of the professionals that he encountered would have jeopardised his position as a foster carer, not least because such patterns of behaviour do not sit easily with the culture favoured by "liberal" professionals. It was therefore not surprising that he struck a different tone in situations where he was more observed by a number of people.

Seeking to control the narrative was not restricted to foster carers. The review relating to an adoptive mother found to have physically abused five children also demonstrated how carers can seek to influence professionals' perceptions through unusual behaviour patterns. The review noted: 'There is some suggestion that Mrs Spry's dominant personality was allowed to drive relationships with the statutory agencies'.

Working the system

Knowledge of the system can place some carers at an advantage. The review relating to four siblings who had been removed from their mother's care because of sexual and physical abuse serves as an example. All four children had been made subject to a care order and placed with foster carers, who then successfully applied for special guardianship orders. Seven years after living with them, one of the boys told of being physically assaulted by the male carer. Six months later, his sister disclosed sexual abuse by one of her brothers. Prior to the children having joined the foster home, there had been a history of foster placements breaking down and an allegation of abuse had been made by a fostered child. Despite this, when these foster carers had applied for special guardianship, the assessment was positive. The review reflected on the carers' ability to influence professional perspectives:

> One of the features of this case was the impact of the SG parents' behaviours in the way they were able to influence decision making. There was evidence of disguised compliance, manipulation and coercion of both professionals and the children in their care by both SG parents. They appeared to "know the system" well.

Dividing professional opinion

Dividing professional opinion and setting one professional group at odds with another can prevent or forestall a comprehensive investigation of concerns and allegations.

In one case, the adoptive mother, Mrs Spry, was skillful in polarising professional opinion so as to avoid practitioners gaining an accurate picture of her parenting. Her having 'alternative views about life and parenting' had been perceived by some professionals as negative, describing her as 'powerful, controlling and generally difficult to work with'. But other professionals had written positively about her, noting her to be 'very caring'. 'A playschool leader described her as having "exceptional parenting skills" and a police officer said that he admired the way she cared for her children.'

The strategy of dividing professional opinion to create obfuscation was found in the review of the siblings A and B. Placed as young children with a relative carer, they had remained in this household until adulthood. At the age of six, the younger sibling A had been assessed as having global developmental delay and attended a specialist school. The relative carer convinced professionals that the older sibling B also had global developmental delay, although not assessed as having any disability and attending mainstream school. There were concerns of harsh parenting and neglect of both children and the scapegoating of sibling B:

> There was the Child in Need meeting where the incident of Sibling B being chained to the radiator was discussed...The school noticed scratches to Sibling B's neck and they contacted the disabled children's team social worker. The school were informed that the relative carer had already explained that the injury was caused accidentally when Sibling B was caught stealing...Further concerns expressed by Sibling A's school about a bruise which the relative carer had said was caused by trying to manage Sibling A's behaviour.

> The schools that the siblings attended became increasingly concerned about their welfare and the attitude of the relative carer to them. They consistently reported those concerns, but their views were dismissed and they were led to believe that they were incorrect in their analysis.

This was in part influenced by the relative carer who sought to split professionals, complaining of having been treated unfairly by school.

CONTROLLING CHILDREN'S NARRATIVE

Perhaps the simplest way for carers to control what children tell professionals is by preventing them from being seen in private. The following case of a boy removed from his birth parents at a very young age due to abuse and neglect, and placed with foster carers, serves as an example. Three years after having been placed, a psychological assessment indicated that the boy 'presented with complex developmental trauma'. Over the next 10 years, he made numerous statements to school staff that his foster carer 'gets mad with him, is nasty to him and did not like him'. He described disturbing morning routines and eating and toileting regimes that raised serious concerns. He failed to gain weight. The school became worried as the foster carer made increasing demands; he 'must change in a separate room for PE and that he was not allowed money for the tuck shop as medical people had advised that he must eat seeds'. Although the boy's behaviour became increasingly disturbed over time, and there were cumulative concerns regarding his physical and emotional well-being, the social worker failed to see him on his own: 'The young person was not routinely seen alone by social workers or by the IRO'.

Abusive carers can develop a strong hold over the children in their household. For example, Mr F (mentioned earlier) had carefully controlled the interactions between the children in his care and the professionals. He attempted, successfully at first, to prevent the children being seen alone. Only after having sought legal advice did he consent to them being seen on their own, but as the review noted, he still managed to control proceedings:

> BD, AD and CD were all seen individually in the house and the chronology notes that Mr F was in the dining room occasionally looking through the door. All the children said that the allegations were not true and they were happy and lucky to be with Mr and Mrs F. The case record notes that social workers were worried that the children had been primed for the interview.

Influencing the child's story was also evident in the following case, where four children had been subjected to non-fatal physical abuse at the hands of their special guardians:

> There were disclosures of physical abuse and subsequent vehement retractions...It later transpired during the court proceedings that the SG [special guardian] parents bribed them with gifts such as televisions for

their bedrooms in order for them to change their stories and support them as their parents.

Blaming the child

A further method that abusive carers used to manipulate professional opinion was to adopt what Sullivan and Quayle (2012) labelled the "suffering manipulation style", in which the perpetrator presents themself as a martyr and emphasises how the problem lies within the child in order to deflect attention from their abusive parenting or lack of care.

"Child blaming" can occur irrespective of the age of the child. For example, a review relating to the death of a 23-month-old boy illustrates this form of manipulation. This young boy had a short and tragic life. Admitted to hospital as a result of injuries sustained whilst in his mother's care, he had been placed with foster carers. Within three months, he was once again admitted to hospital and died from non-accidental injuries inflicted on him by his foster mother. The review highlighted the ability of carers to mislead professionals:

> *That professionals could be so convinced that there was "something wrong" with T and the problem was with him, is an indication of the level of deviousness to which the foster carers resorted to ensure that their neglect and ill treatment of T remained undiscovered, until it was too late.*

The issue of "child blaming" was also found in cases involving older children. One example is the case of two siblings looked after by a relative carer, where one suffered global developmental delay (discussed earlier):

> *Much of what is written about them in the assessments and records is reported directly by the relative carer with who they lived and was often negative and derogatory in nature.*

There were numerous incidents when one or other of the siblings had made disclosures about abuse and neglect. The carer always acknowledged that the incident had happened, 'but that the actions had been necessary because of the complex and destructive behaviour of the siblings; in effect the adults blamed the siblings for the harm they had experienced'.

Fabricating or inducing illness

> *Fabricated or induced illness (FII) is a rare form of child abuse. It occurs when a parent or carer, usually the child's biological mother, exaggerates or deliberately causes symptoms of illness in the child.*

(NHS, 2019)

In 2008, the Government published supplementary guidance to provide a national framework within which agencies and professionals work together to protect children in cases where illness may be fabricated or induced (FII) (DCSF, 2008).

Although the syndrome is uncommon, FII is associated with significant mortality, physical illness and disability. An overview of case reports (Sheridan, 2003) concluded that six per cent of cases resulted in death, and in 7.3 per cent of cases, the child experienced long-term or permanent injury.

The case of Mrs Spry, the adoptive mother of five children, provides an example of how practitioners may have failed to identify fabricated or induced illness. The review noted that at different times:

> Mrs Spry claimed that three of the children suffered Attention Deficit Hyperactivity Disorder (ADHD) or Attention Deficit Disorder and later that Carol suffered with Autistic Spectrum Disorder...There was evidence of degrees of uncertainty in respect of the diagnoses of ADHD for all the children, and that Mrs Spry always spoke for the children, never let them be seen alone, and Ritalin was prescribed for excessive periods of time without the children being seen. Mrs Spry was insistent on the need for treatment and sought out private clinics, without agreement of the GP, to get a diagnosis to support the need for treatment. On one occasion the GP noted an allegation (not known from whom) that Mrs Spry had been giving Belinda Valium, obtained from a neighbour.

Following a car accident, Belinda became wheelchair-bound 'despite there being no apparent physical reason...After leaving Mrs Spry's care, Belinda quickly regained her mobility'.

The review noted that the possibility of fabricated or induced illness had never been raised formally as a concern by any of the professionals involved with the children.

SUMMARY OF KEY FINDINGS

- Abuse and neglect can have a profound and long-lasting impact on children. The strategies used to cope successfully with frightening situations in the past may present a challenge to current carers. Professionals working with children living with foster carers, adopters and special guardians face the challenge of balancing the needs of carers for support with ensuring that children are cared for, protected and thrive. In order to do this, professionals should not assume children who have been "rescued" from an abusive or neglectful home are safe with their current carers – placements may not be safe places.

- When carers behave in neglectful or abusive ways towards the children in their care, they may utilise a range of methods to avoid professional oversight. The most comprehensive is to severely restrict children's contact with the outside world, through, for example, home schooling and a failure to register children with GP services. When children are not taken to or do not attend medical appointments on a regular basis, this should be followed up robustly rather than result in the service being withdrawn.

- Carers may seek to avoid scrutiny by removing children from school. At present, there is no statutory duty to monitor home education on a routine basis. However, guidance by the Department for Education was issued in April 2019 to help local authorities understand their role in relation to elective home education (Department for Education, 2019a; Foster and Danechi, 2019).

- Carers may also seek to deflect professional scrutiny through misleading behaviour, a concept reported as disguised compliance, and first recorded by Reder and colleagues (1993). Disguised compliance is the apparent willingness to co-operate with agreed plans that are not followed through and is used as a way to keep practitioners at a distance. Establishing the facts and gathering information is essential to understanding what is actually going on. Professionals should not unquestioningly accept presenting behaviour, excuses or reassurances that carers have changed or will change how they care for the children.

- Creating confusion among professionals by presenting different personae is another method used by carers to deflect scrutiny. When professionals have a long and positive history of working with particular carers, shifting perceptions when concerns are raised can be difficult. Talking to other professionals and to the child alone to co-ordinate information about the family will provide a fuller picture of what life is like for children in the household.

- Fabricated or induced illness is rare, and the Government guidance (DCSF, 2008) acknowledges the complexity of the assessment task. Practitioners must consider the impact of the carer's behaviour on the child and balance the natural worries of a concerned carer with the possibility that the illness or disability is being fabricated.

- Carers may also seek to influence professionals' opinions in a variety of ways. They may build up a history of active co-operation and a willingness to agree with every request to place a child with them. Those with very dominant personalities may drive the discourse and influence professional decision-making in their favour.

- Perhaps most concerning is the extent to which carers can control both direct access to the children they look after and the information children disclose. A child's allegation may be retracted for numerous reasons, including carers' bribes, fear of retribution, lack of trust in professionals, or a dread of the unknown and further upheavals.

- The greatest challenge professionals face is to "think the unthinkable", to focus on the protection and welfare of the child and ensure that their voices are heard and their stories are known. The practitioner's task is to uncover what life is like for a child in a particular household. To accomplish this trust is essential – it cannot be rushed and takes time to establish.

Chapter 7
Everybody's responsibility

Everyone who works with children has a responsibility for keeping them safe. No single practitioner can have a full picture of a child's needs and circumstances and, if children and families are to receive the right help at the right time, everyone who comes into contact with them has a role to play in identifying concerns, sharing information and taking prompt action.

(HM Government, 2018, p.10, para 16)

THE COMPLEXITY OF CASES

One of the most striking features of many of the serious case reviews in this study is the complexity of the cases and the number of different professionals involved. As a result of the abuse and neglect children have experienced, they may need to engage with a range of practitioners, including social workers; health professionals (GPs, health visitors or Child and Adolescent Mental Health Services (CAMHS) professionals); early years' providers; teaching professionals (teachers, year heads, pastoral care teachers, special needs teachers, deputy and head teachers and virtual school heads); police; youth offending teams; probation; children's guardians; and the voluntary sector. Add to this the professionals working with the foster carer, adopter or special guardian, and the numbers increase. Different health professionals (GPs, mental health and hospital services); fostering social workers; in some cases drug and alcohol services; police; probation; and voluntary sector services may be involved. Furthermore, over time and with numerous children living in a household, the number of practitioners with some knowledge of the family circumstances increases exponentially. One review noted:

The information provided for this review is extensive and covers sixteen years of involvement with the foster carers and the six children who are subjects of the review. Six hundred and thirty-five professionals have been identified during the review process as having some involvement with the case.

This is the context, in some cases, in which agencies and professionals attempt to carry out their duty to work together to safeguard and promote the welfare of children.

The consequences of ineffective collaboration between different professionals and agencies have been consistently recorded in child protection research and identified in triennial serious case reviews (see, for example, Brandon *et al*, 2020). Colin Green suggests that:

> *...the main reason co-operation is difficult is that exhortation to co-operate does not solve the problem that those working with looked after children have different roles, interests and priorities. These differences are professional, structural, related to policy, and, on occasions, value-based.*

> (Green, 2019, p.4)

The current study shines a spotlight on the array of different professionals who may need to collaborate in a single case. It identifies missed opportunities to record information, to understand its significance, and to share the information in a timely manner.

Where agencies include different teams or different front-line organisations, poor information sharing can occur both within and between agencies. This was evident in many of the serious case reviews and particularly within the health service.

COMMUNICATION WITHIN THE HEALTH SERVICE

The Government is committed to 'making all patient and care records digital, real-time and interoperable by 2020'. A staged approach has been taken:

> *By 2018, this record will include information from all their health and care interactions...By the end of 2018, all doctors and nurses will be able to access the most up-to-date lifesaving information across GP surgeries, ambulance services and A&E departments, no matter where a patient is in England.*

> (House of Commons Library, 2016, p.4)

Research on the progress of implementing the electronic health records has highlighted difficulties in implementation (see, for example, research by the Centre for Public Impact, 2017, and The King's Fund study by Honeyman *et al*, 2016).

> *Provided that certain conditions (mainly related to interoperability) are met, using digital health records should allow the whole record (or relevant information from it) to be shared quickly, securely and in a standard way between health professionals to support patient care,*

*forming an "integrated" electronic health record. The complex mix
of systems and practices in the NHS at present means that this is not
happening as often as it could.*

(Honeyman *et al*, 2016, p.8)

Although implementation is slower than originally envisioned, the delays
and frustrations have not diminished the strong support from NHS
clinicians for electronic health records (Robertson *et al*, 2010).

The introduction of electronic health records should enable all
health practitioners to gain a complete picture of a child's health and
development. The reviews of historic cases pre-date the introduction of
this system and the more recent reviews suggest that implementation
of an electronic record was still in its infancy at the time. The following
case illustrates the disadvantages of not having an electronic record.

> *The evidence suggests in this case that there is no one electronic health
> record for the child that all health professionals can access. The GP, the
> health visitor, the registrar and the paediatricians all had some medical
> information but not all the information. This did not promote any of the
> health professionals having a full picture of the child's health.*

The inability of health professionals to access each others' records was
an issue highlighted in the case of Faith, a 15-month-old foster child.
The foster carers had reported to a minor illness nurse that Faith had a
swollen forearm. The nurse 'recorded a slight discoloration to the wrist,
similar to bruising, advised treatment with Calpol and to return if there
was no improvement within 24 hours'. Four days later, the foster mother
repeated her concerns to the visiting community nursery nurse, telling
her 'she had consulted her GP, who was not worried...Neither the health
visitor nor the community nursery nurse had direct access to GP records
and therefore were unable to confirm GP consultations'. Two months
later, Faith was admitted to hospital with eight separate limb fractures
that were deemed to be non-accidental injuries.

Similar issues arose in the case of a six-month baby placed with foster
carers. The baby was:

> *...examined under LSCB procedures on two occasions in February 2008,
> whilst in the new foster placement...The results of the skeletal survey
> were not communicated to the paediatrician until three weeks after the
> x-rays had been undertaken. The results of the skeletal survey revealed
> Baby Z had fractures to one arm.*

The lack of information sharing within the health service was also a key
theme identified in the following serious case review:

> *Between the various disciplines within health, there were a number of
> opportunities when information sharing could have been better: between
> maternity services and the health visitor; between the health visitor and*

GP; between the radiologist and paediatrician; and between the health visitor and paediatrician. Whilst each discipline followed child protection procedures rigorously, they did so within the limits and structures of their own discipline and not between the different health disciplines, or effectively enough with other external agencies.

The introduction of electronic health records will not be a panacea to all the difficulties with regard to sharing information. A possible stumbling block may be the new NHS number and medical record that is now mandatory for adopted children. It should, however, when fully implemented, enable health professionals to gain a more complete picture of a child's health history and thus more fully understand their circumstances.

Children with disabilities

There is little research on the outcomes for looked after children with disabilities. What does exist suggests that educational as well as behavioural and emotional outcomes are more negative than outcomes for looked after children generally (Kelly *et al*, 2012). Perhaps the most obvious difference is that a child with disabilities is likely to have a greater number of professionals involved in their life – professionals who all need to communicate effectively with each other.

The case of M provides an example. The review described M's main health needs as:

- *Severe short stature (at the time of her death aged 11 she had the height of typical 2–3-year-old);*

- *Severe visual handicap; and*

- *Severe learning difficulties causing delayed development.*

A respite arrangement with foster carer W had been made for M, which had enabled her to live with her birth family 'for as long as her mother wanted to care for her'. Once this was no longer possible, W became her long-term carer. M died two years later while on holiday with W and other members of W's family. The post mortem examination found that the death had resulted from a ruptured liver caused by an inflicted injury. 'Police enquiries showed no concerning circumstances surrounding the death and the police subsequently decided that there were no grounds for a criminal prosecution in relation to the cause of M's death.'

The review gave a positive report of her life with her foster carers:

She had been cared for in family settings throughout her life and been encouraged to lead as active a life as her disability allowed, while being closely supervised: the consensus was that it had been good that M had been given such opportunities and that her quality of life had been as good as it could, given her severe disability.

The review also found that health professionals had worked well with one another and that 'the lead clinician from the Royal Free Hospital and the Designated Doctor for Looked After Children played a valuable role in ensuring that information was shared appropriately'.

However, prior to coming into care, when M was still living at home and receiving respite care, information sharing had been less adequate. The agencies that had provided reports for the serious case review made recommendations which included the importance of improved communication and information sharing. For example, the primary care trust report made recommendations in relation to:

- *improved communication between hospital consultants, the child's social workers and the Looked After Children's (LAC) Consultant after hospital consultations;*

- *the need for improved liaison between social services and GPs when a child is moved to a new foster carer for long-term care;*

- *the need to agree a clear definition of the remit of the "lead clinician" for a child with a disability and ensure that it is universally understood.*

COLLABORATION BETWEEN HEALTH, EDUCATION AND CHILDREN'S SOCIAL CARE

There were many examples in the serious case reviews of good practice where health, education and children's social care had worked collaboratively and shared information to support the child. In other cases, the process had not worked so well.

The review relating to the case of a six-year-old boy, Child 1, showed how this can arise because professionals lacked an understanding of what information 'can be shared, what can be shared verbally and what needs to be requested in writing'. A 14-year-old boy was then placed with the same foster carers and went on to sexually abuse Child 1. Soon after the older boy had joined the household, Child 1's behaviour at school deteriorated. The change in household membership had not been shared with the school:

> *There's no formal process for sharing changes to the child's placement by introduction of other members to the household with the school.*

Similarly, information held by the school about the changes in Child 1's behaviour had not been shared with health professionals or children's social care. As a result, no link was made between the changes in behaviour noted by the school and the introduction to the household of the older boy.

A further example of poor joint working is illustrated by the case of Child B who had been placed with a foster family at birth. At the age of eight months, B had moved to live with prospective adopters. During the following two weeks, the prospective adoptive mother had taken B to hospital with injuries on two occasions. Two days after the second hospital visit, the adopters had rung 999 'because Child B had stopped breathing'. A post mortem found that she had a fractured skull and widespread bruising.

The review noted gaps in the assessment, reports and records and a general lack of management oversight. At the point of the pre-birth child protection conference, no invitation had been sent to health professionals. This was a significant gap and the lack of inclusion of key professionals was replicated across the whole period under review.

INFORMATION SHARING BETWEEN CHILDREN'S AND FOSTERING SOCIAL WORK TEAMS

Several of the reviews noted good practice, where information had been shared in a timely manner between the social worker responsible for the child and the fostering social worker (also referred to as the supervising social worker). The following is one such example, noting:

> ...the sensitive planning by fostering staff and the children's social workers regarding placement choice for some of the children when they had to move between placements.

Unfortunately, this was not always the case. One of many cases is that of two-year-old Child T, placed with foster carers. This little boy had experienced non-accidental injuries inflicted by his mother and was under an interim care order when in hospital. He had been taken directly from hospital and placed with foster carers; tragically, Child T died three months later. During the child's time with these carers, three social workers, as well as social workers from the emergency duty team, and the fostering social worker had been involved. The review noted that 'it was the fostering social worker, of all the social care professionals, who had the most consistent contact with him during this three-month period'. Unfortunately, the fostering social worker had not been invited to the LAC review, and as a result had not been part of the subsequent meetings involving family and professionals. This oversight was 'seemingly not queried by the Independent Reviewing Officer'.

The review concluded that the failure to share information ran through the history of this case:

A further significant finding of the review is that there was a pattern of not sharing information between professionals throughout this case, which sadly contributed to the serious outcome for Child T.

Other reviews identified the possible impact on a child's safety when professionals have conflicting perceptions or are not involved in the assessment process. In one case, Child B and her brother had been placed as young children with a single female foster carer. When the girl was 10 years old, her brother had told his teacher that he had seen her being sexually abused by the 19-year-old adopted son of their carer, who was subsequently arrested and charged with rape. The NSPCC was commissioned to carry out an independent assessment of the needs of all the children and the capacity of the carer to provide a safe environment. The recommendation was that Child B and her brother remain with the carer but the other three children in the household were to be moved to an alternative placement.

The review highlighted strong differences of opinion between the fostering social worker and childcare social worker; these concerned the standards of hygiene within the carer's home and 'her ability to cope satisfactorily with the care of the many children in the household, and the large numbers of cats and dogs, the farm animals and her various employments'. The conflicting opinions had not been resolved and led to a 'lack of clarity over what should be expected and whether there was a need for action to address the concerns'. The case review panel found that while such circumstances did not suggest that the abuse was predictable, 'abuse and neglect are more likely to occur in households that are chaotic and lack adequate supervision and clear boundaries'.

These illustrations, drawn from a number of serious case reviews, show how a lack of communication and collaboration between the social worker responsible for the child and the fostering social work team, whose responsibility is to provide support to foster carers, can compromise a joint approach to meeting the needs of looked after children. The illustrations do not, however, support the recommendations put forward in a recent review for the DfE, in which the authors, Narey and Owers, propose rationalising the professional supervision of foster placements by allowing local authorities to 'decide which individual social worker is best placed to offer the support to the foster family in long-term placements' (Narey and Owers, 2018, p.101, para 6). This proposal was at odds with the views of The Fostering Network (2018). The serious case reviews included in this study would suggest that there is still a strong argument for maintaining the separation of the role of the supervising social worker from that of the child's social worker. An international literature review also supports the distinctive role of the supervising social worker, which is much appreciated by foster carers (Brown *et al*, 2014).

COLLABORATION IN ADOPTION, SPECIAL GUARDIANSHIP AND KINSHIP CARE

When children are adopted, subject to special guardianship orders or child arrangements orders, the responsibility of the local authority ceases. No reviews are held and therefore there is no formal arena for sharing information. This lack of information sharing once an order is made was highlighted in the review relating to Shi-Anne. When placed with her relative and after the special guardianship order was granted, this toddler 'was almost invisible to professionals'. The subsequent change in status for the child had not been shared with key professionals such as the GP and health visitor.

The removal of local authority oversight once a special guardianship order is granted, and the lack of a formal structure for professionals to share information, was also an issue identified in the following serious case review. Two-year-old Bonnie was living with her maternal grandmother on a special guardianship order and the case was closed by children's social care. The review noted that the involvement of health visitors and GPs was fragmented and key information lost. The failure to share information was highlighted in the review, following an incident where Bonnie fell from her pushchair into the canal:

> *The absence of a lead multi-agency worker, either through a Common Assessment Framework or at the statutory level of Child in Need, was a significant barrier to effective information sharing and multi-agency risk assessment at this point.*

The lack of an official arena for sharing concerns was also identified in relation to the death of Child J, a seven-year-old girl who lived with her aunt under a special guardianship order. The review recorded poor information-sharing in relation to assessment and support planning:

> *The absence of any plan for the placement with Aunt meant there was a lack of a multi-agency approach, and no professional or agency questioned this. Neither health nor education were included in the SGO assessment or support planning and so were unaware of what the implications of the SGO were for their provision of services to Child J.*

Similar concerns over inadequate information-sharing and collaborative working were noted in serious case reviews relating to children placed for adoption. In the case of a toddler, the review identified numerous missed opportunities to share information and concerns about the baby's safety and welfare:

> *The sharing of information between the child's social worker and the adoption social worker following the child's fall down the stairs did not take place until three weeks after the incident.*

The child was presented to the GP with a unilateral squint. There is no evidence this was formally shared with Children's Services.

There is no evidence of any formal record from Health to Children's Services regarding the child's presentations to hospital following injury.

The child, while still legally a child looked after, was considered an adopted child and so this shaped the way in which professionals shared information.

There is clearly a need for a multi-agency set of professional standards for children who are placed for adoption or on special guardianship orders that includes what is expected regarding the sharing of information.

INFORMATION SHARING BETWEEN CHILDREN AND ADULT SERVICES

The very complexity and co-morbidity of some cases will result in the need for collaboration between services for adults, such as domestic abuse, substance misuse and mental illness, and those working with children. Research has identified that a major organisational barrier to effective information sharing and joint working is the different understanding of confidentiality and data protection held by various professionals and agencies (Cleaver *et al*, 2011).

The reviews identified a number of cases where professionals preferred to work within the "comfort zone" of their own specialism. The review of a case of historical sexual abuse noted that the male foster carer, Mr F, had mental health issues. Unfortunately, the information about his difficulties had not been shared and did not inform any evaluation of the placement or the possible impact on the children in the household:

There was no communication between the GP and social workers, and mental health professionals did not consider the implications of Mr F's symptoms on his capacity to parent.

The review relating to Bonnie, a two-year-old girl living with her grandmother under a special guardianship order, provides a further example. The child's mother, who had been living in a tent and subject to domestic abuse, moved with her abusive boyfriend to live with her baby daughter in her own mother's home. This was contrary to the safeguards agreed with the court and with children's social care, and 'should have raised fresh concerns for immediate action by the local authority'. The review noted that the case management of the child's mother 'was entirely separate and disconnected from any consideration or concerns for her child'.

Collaboration with adult services would enable children's social workers to gain a better understanding of how the issues affecting parents and carers, such as depression, substance misuse or domestic abuse, impact on carers and family functioning. It is essential that information is shared between adult services and children's services to ensure that child protection conferences and reviews have all the relevant information when making plans or considering whether plans are still suitable.

POLICE AND YOUTH OFFENDING TEAMS (YOTS) NOT "IN THE LOOP"

> *Protecting children is one of the most important tasks the police undertake. Every officer and member of police staff should understand his or her duty to protect children as part of his or her day-to-day business.*

(HMICFRS, 2015, p.5)

> *To be effective YOTs must successfully straddle the criminal justice system and children's and wider youth services. YOTs must have a foot firmly planted in both camps to bridge the gap between the two.*

(Youth Justice Board, 2015, p.5, para 1.9)

A 16-year-old boy, D, had died from a drug overdose. He had been privately fostered for nine years before a residence order was made. The review noted a number of instances where agencies had not worked together to ensure his safety and welfare. From the age of 11, he had not attended school and refused home tuition. Although outside the educational services, he was well known to the police. The Youth Offending Team (YOT), however, did not perceive his criminal activity to be related to child protection issues and relevant information was not shared:

> *The Youth Offending Team had involvement with D because of his criminal activities and anti-social behaviour. There was no liaison or sharing of information between the Youth Offending Team and health, police and social services agencies. Contact with education and training agencies did not lead to sharing anxieties regarding his safety and welfare.*

The review found that D received a comprehensive lack of support, despite admissions of self-harm and other disordered behaviour. Agencies had also not recognised the damage caused by a chronic lack of education.

A CO-ORDINATED APPROACH FOR CHILDREN OF ASYLUM SEEKERS AND UNACCOMPANIED ASYLUM-SEEKING CHILDREN

An unaccompanied child is entitled to the same local authority support as any other looked after child, and our ambitions for these children are the same: to have a safe and stable placement, to receive the care that they need to thrive, and the support they need to fulfil their educational and other outcomes.

(DfE, 2017b, p.9)

The Government has produced non-statutory guidance for agencies working with unaccompanied asylum-seeking children. This identifies the need to share information in order to ensure that a child is safe from harm:

In assessing the needs of UASC[1] and providing effective care local authorities will normally need to build close links with the UKBA[2] "case owner" responsible for resolving the child's immigration status. This should extend to sharing key information necessary to safeguard the child's welfare.

(HM Government, 2010b, p.320, para 11.115)

In some cases, despite following the correct procedures and agencies working constructively together, tragedy cannot be avoided. This is illustrated by the serious case review into the death of an unaccompanied asylum-seeking boy of 17 years. YT arrived from Eritrea concealed in a lorry transporting wheelie bins. He was arrested in London, placed under police protection and later in emergency foster care. The police initially questioned his age but the boy spoke no English and an online translation service was used to communicate. YT became very frustrated and as a result he 'punched a wall in the interview room', which led to him being placed in handcuffs. The emergency duty team in children's social care arranged for an emergency placement and the police took him to the foster carers' home. The following evening, he was found by his carers to have committed suicide by hanging.

The review found evidence of professionals taking a sensitive approach, but highlighted that police enquiries had focused on verifying the boy's age rather than finding out his wishes and feelings, which might have assisted a wider assessment of need. It was acknowledged that 'there was no guarantee for the professionals that additional probing of what was an already tired and unsettled young person would add much to their understanding of his needs'. The review concluded that there was

---

1   Unaccompanied asylum-seeking children

2   United Kingdom Border Agency

'almost nothing to suggest to any professional or carer that YT was a suicide risk'.

The following review was less positive in its findings. The focus was an asylum seeker from China, who made a private fostering arrangement for her baby after her asylum claim had been rejected. A few months later, the baby was admitted to hospital not breathing, cold and unresponsive. The case echoes the findings from a recent qualitative study that found many children who presented as "privately fostered" had, in effect, been abandoned by their parents and were living with strangers (Wells, 2019).

The serious case review panel in this case 'considered that a more robust and inclusive multi-agency approach was needed to identifying and meeting the needs of asylum-seeking children and the children of asylum seekers and failed asylum seekers'.

It goes on to recommend that:

> ...whenever a parent suggests to any agency relinquishing their child for adoption or giving their child into the care of unrelated "others", this should automatically trigger a referral to Social Care for a core assessment in order to explore the motivation behind the plan and ensure the child is adequately safeguarded.

More recently, the Home Office has produced guidance for Home Office staff in relation to children seeking asylum, some of whom are privately fostered:

> If there are immediate and/or significant concerns, for example about the fostering or care arrangements, Home Office staff must refer the case immediately to the social worker.

(Home Office, 2019, p.20)

THE ROLE OF PROFESSIONALS IN ESCALATING CONCERNS

Section 11 of the Children Act 2004 places a duty on organisations and agencies to have arrangements that reflect the importance of safeguarding and promoting the welfare of children. Included in this are 'clear escalation policies for staff to follow when their child safeguarding concerns are not being addressed within their organisation or by other agencies' (HM Government, 2018).

Several of the reviews identified professional confusion and uncertainty over their agency's escalation policy. The following case provides an example.

Child R had been born unaided at the mother's home, after a concealed pregnancy. On discharge from hospital, mother and baby went to live with the child's grandparents. The health visitor recorded concerns about the mother's parenting, the very poor home conditions and the child's failure to gain weight. A hospital stay established that there was no medical reason for the child's failure to gain weight:

> *The health visitor discussed her concerns about Child R and the lack of action by CSF [Children, Schools and Families] with the safeguarding nurse on two occasions. Whilst the safeguarding nurse did pursue these matters rigorously at the time, neither she nor the HV [health visitor] persisted in escalating their concerns further when they received a poor response.*

The review noted that the arrangements for escalating concerns 'were not sufficiently effective in this case and should be reviewed to ensure identified risk and concerns are acted upon promptly'.

A review relating to a 14-year-old girl with a history of mental health difficulties, including suicidal ideation, also highlighted the consequences of not escalating concerns. The girl had been the subject of four LAC reviews and had the same IRO throughout, who was committed to understanding her and establishing her views. However, when the IRO found that her recommendations had not been implemented, there was no effective response. The review concluded with the following statement. 'Escalation and challenge are clearly important tenets of the LAC system, the absence of which compromises effective care planning for children.' Sadly, this young teenage girl took her own life.

A CHANGE OF LOCAL AUTHORITY

> *Local authorities placing children in another local authority area are required to notify the host authority prior to placement.*
>
> (HM Government, 2010b, p.294, para 11.7)

> *All practitioners should be particularly alert to the importance of sharing information when a child moves from one local authority into another, due to the risk that knowledge pertinent to keeping a child safe could be lost.*
>
> (HM Government, 2018, p.18, para 2)

In a number of the cases reviewed, children had been moved from one local authority area to another. For example, the review relating to LH, a four-year-old boy, also highlighted how information about a child can be lost when a case is transferred from one local authority area to another: 'It is a familiar theme in serious case reviews that those children who move from one borough to another do not always receive a seamless service.'

The review noted that practitioners in the original borough 'thought there was a supervision order in place in respect of LH (there was not)... An SGO support plan (ratified by the court) was in place, supplemented by Child in Need procedures to support LH's transition'. Despite this, there were no multi-agency meetings to facilitate the transfer and ensure that information was passed on to the relevant professionals. 'The pre-school and (later) school he attended had no knowledge of the extent of the neglect he had suffered or the meaning of a SGO.'

The tragic case of P, a teenage boy, who died from a drug overdose, serves as a further example. P had experienced numerous placement breakdowns and a brief period in a children's home during his seven years in care. A further placement breakdown resulted in P, now 15 years old, being placed with yet another set of foster carers at very short notice. Shortly after P's arrival, a different local authority placed a 15-year-old boy, with a serious drug habit, in the same foster home. The boys did not get on and P's behaviour deteriorated. The review made the following conclusion:

> It appears that details of the other child's problems and needs were never provided to P's social workers and managers – the individual and agencies who held this information each seem to be of the opinion that this was the responsibility of the other, or of [the current local authority] to ask for the information.

There appeared to be no set procedure in place to ensure that when a child moved from one local authority to another, all relevant information would be transferred.

SUMMARY OF KEY FINDINGS

- A challenge to a timely and co-ordinated approach to information sharing is the large number of professionals who may be involved in a single family looking after a number of unrelated children. In addition to the range of universal services the family has access to, such as health, education, police and social services, they may also have contact with specialist services. These could include services for adults as well as for children. The number of professionals working with the family rises significantly when a child has a disability. Effective and timely information sharing can be enhanced when there is a lead professional as contact point and co-ordinator.

- To understand whether a child presenting with a physical injury has been harmed, health practitioners need to know the medical history of the child and family. This requires practitioners to be able to access each others' records. At present, this is not always possible and decisions are made on the basis of incomplete information. The Government has introduced the use of electronic health records; once successfully implemented, they should help to overcome this barrier.

- There were many examples of different agencies working collaboratively and sharing information in a timely manner. However, in some cases, information did not always get shared appropriately. Despite Government guidance and inter-agency protocols, practitioners held different understandings of what can be shared and how information should be transmitted. Protocols for information sharing are important but so too is the development of formal processes for this to be carried out.

- When a child is being placed for special guardianship, there is no official arena for sharing information. The information held by statutory agencies such as health and education does not necessarily inform assessments or support planning. There is a need for multi-agency protocols and guidance to be developed in relation to children in these circumstances.

- Practitioners working with adults tend to focus on their own client and do not always appreciate the impact that, for example, mental health problems, domestic abuse or substance misuse may have on their client's parenting capacity. A greater emphasis on joint training with children's welfare professionals and collaborative work should enable professionals to understand the wider implications of their client's difficulties and ensure that the information they hold informs assessments and plans for looked after children.

- With regard to asylum-seeking children, there is clear guidance for the police, Youth Offending Teams and the Home Office in relation to working in partnership with children's services. Nonetheless, some cases in this study revealed no liaison or sharing of information between these services and children's social care. Once again, joint training, local protocols and formal processes should support greater understanding of the value of collaborative working.

- Fostering households will have both a supervising social worker and a children's social worker involved with the family. In the majority of cases, these practitioners work very effectively together to support the family and ensure that children are safe and thrive. Although escalation polices, applicable to all professions, exist to resolve strongly-held differences of opinion, the reviews identified a degree of confusion and uncertainty over how and when these should be activated.

- When children move from one local authority to another, information about them and their circumstances can be lost. It is essential that there are processes for sharing information and a clear understanding over who has responsibility for ensuring that this is done in a timely manner.

Conclusion

It is essential that the findings from child abuse research are widely disseminated and influence practice. This study of 52 local safeguarding reviews has identified recurring themes that have posed challenges and dilemmas for practitioners in carrying out their responsibilities to children living with adopters, foster carers or special guardians. It is hoped that the evidence from this study will contribute to the "learning culture", that many organisations safeguarding and promoting the welfare of children, are striving to achieve.

In order to make knowledge from the study more readily accessible to those in practice, the findings have informed the development of a companion short guide. The guide, *Safeguarding Children Living with Foster Carers*, *Adopters and Special Guardians: A guide to reflective practice*, summarises the research and examines five basic themes emerging from this study:

- assessing and selecting carers;

- ensuring children's welfare, safety and nurture;

- supporting carers;

- maintaining respectful uncertainty;

- collaborating in the interests of the child.

Within each theme, the challenges facing practitioners have been explored, and practitioners are presented with a series of questions. These have been designed to encourage reflection, prompt action, and act as an "aide memoire". It is not a comprehensive set of practice guidelines, but has been developed with the knowledge from the study to assist the far-reaching judgements professionals are required to make.

A range of different practitioners will be involved in safeguarding children. The companion guide, although primarily aimed at social workers and managers, holds relevant information for associated health, education, police and other professionals who work alongside children's social workers.

References

Adoption UK (2017) *Adoption UK's Schools & Exclusion Report*, available at: www.adoptionuk.org/Handlers/Download.ashx?IDMF=f67b07f1-710c-4087-a737-fc5264b0c063

Adoption UK (2019) *The Adoption Barometer*, available at: www.adoptionuk.org

Adullah MQ (2018) 'Gender differences in learning disabled children', *Neuropsychological Review Research and Review on Health Care*, 1:3

BAAF/New Family Social (2013) *Lesbian and Gay Adoption and Fostering – social workers*, London: BAAF

Baginsky M, Gorin S and Sands C (2017) *The Fostering System in England: Evidence review*, DfE Research Report, DFE-RB679, available at: www.gov.uk/government/publications/the-fostering-system-in-england-review

Barnardo's (2020) *Barnardo's declares 'State of Emergency' as Number of Children needing Foster Care during the Coronavirus Pandemic rises by 44%*, available at: www.barnardos.org.uk

BECOME (2018) *Letter to Children's Minister, Nadhim Zahawi MP, Regarding Fostering Stocktake Recommendations*, available at: www.becomecharity.org.uk

Biehal N, Cusworth L, Wade J and Clarke S (2014) *Keeping Children Safe: Allegations concerning the abuse or neglect of children in care*, London: University of York and NSPCC, available at: www.nspcc.org.uk

Borthwick S and Lord D (2019) *Effective Fostering Panels*, London: CoramBAAF

Brandon M, Bailey S, Belderson P, Gardner R, Sidebotham P, Dodsworth J, Warren C and Black J (2009) *Understanding Serious Case Reviews and their Impact: A biennial analysis of serious case reviews 2005–07*, London: DCSF

Brandon M, Sidebotham P, Belderson P, Cleaver H, Dickens J, Garstang J, Harris J, Sorensen P and Wate R (2020) *Complexity & Challenge: A triennial review of SCRs 2014–2017*, available at: https://assets.publishing.service.gov.uk/government/uploads/system/uploads/attachment_data/file/869586/TRIENNIAL_SCR_REPORT_2014_to_2017.pdf

Brazier M (2019) *Fostering: What do the latest statistics tell us?*, available at: www.socialcareinspection.blog.gov.uk/2019/02/15/fostering

Brown HC, Sebba J and Luke N (2014) *The Role of the Supervising Social Worker in Foster Care*, available at: www.education.ox.ac.uk/wp-content/uploads/2019/05/285261.pdf

Care Crisis Review (2018) *Options for Change*, London: Family Rights Group

Care Inspectorate (2013) *A Report into the Deaths of Looked After Children in Scotland 2009–2011*, available at: www.careinspectorate.com

Care Inspectorate (2016) *Learning from Significant Case Reviews in Scotland 1 April 2012–31 March 2015*, available at: www.careinspectorate.com

Care Inspectorate (2019) *Learning from Significant Case Reviews in Scotland March 2015–April 2018*, available at: www.careinspectorate.com

Chapman R (2019) *Undertaking a Fostering Assessment in England* (3rd edn), London, CoramBAAF

Centre for Public Impact (2017) *The Electronic Health Records System*, available at: www.centreforpublicimpact.org

Chesterfield T (2012) *Local Authority's Actions in Relation to Children in Foster Care Declared Unlawful under UK Human Rights Act*, Human Rights Case Summaries, available at: www.bailii.org/

Children's Commissioner (2019) *Childhood Vulnerability in Numbers*, available at: www.childrenscommissioner.gov.uk

Cleaver H, Unell I and Aldgate J (2011) *Children's Needs – Parenting Capacity. Child abuse: Parental mental illness, learning disability, substance misuse, and domestic violence* (2nd edn), London: The Stationery Office

Cmd. 6636 (1945) *Report by Sir Walter Monckton on the circumstances that led to the boarding out of Dennis and Terence O'Neill at Bank Farm, Minsterley, and the steps taken to supervise their welfare*, London: HMSO

Cmd. 6922 (1946) *Report of the Care of Children Committee*. London: HMSO

CoramBAAF (2015) *Special Guardianship, Kinship Care and Private Fostering*, available at: www.corambaaf.org.uk

CoramBAAF (2019) *Prospective Foster Carer Report (Form F): Guidance Notes*, available at: www.corambaaf.org.uk

Courts and Tribunals Judiciary (2019) *Family Justice Council: Interim Guidance on Special Guardianship*, available at: www.judiciary.uk/wp-content/uploads/2019/05/fjc-sg-intrim-guidance-pdf-approved-draft-21-may-2019-1.pdf

De Jong A and Donnelly S (2015) *Recruiting, Assessing and Supporting Lesbian and Gay Adopters*, London: BAAF

Department for Children, Schools and Families (2008) *Safeguarding Children in Whom Illness is Fabricated or Induced*, London: DCSF

Department for Children, Schools and Families (2009) *Safeguarding Disabled Children: Practice guidance*, London: DCSF

Department for Children, Schools and Families (2010) *Statutory Guidance for Independent Reviewing Officers and Local Authorities on their Functions in Relation to Case Management and Review for Looked After Children*, London: DCSF

Department for Education (2010) *Family and Friends Care: Statutory guidance for local authorities*, available at: https://assets.publishing. service.gov.uk/government/uploads/system/uploads/attachment_data/ file/288483/family-and-friends-care.pdf

Department for Education (2011) *Fostering Services: National minimum standards*, available at: https://assets.publishing.service.gov.uk/ government/uploads/system/uploads/attachment_data/file/192705/ NMS_Fostering_Services.pdf

Department for Education (2013a) *Statutory Guidance on Adoption*, DFE-00126-2013, available at: www.gov.uk/government/publications/ adoption-statutory-guidance-2013

Department for Education (2013b) *Assessment and Approval of Foster Carers: Amendments to the Children Act 1989 Guidance and Regulations*, available at: www.gov.uk

Department for Education (2014) *Children in Care*, available at: www.nao.org.uk/report/children-in-care/

Department for Education (2015) *Special Guardianship Review: Report on findings*, available at: www.gov.uk/government/consultations/special-guardianship-review

Department for Education (2017a) *Special Guardianship Guidance*, available at: https://assets.publishing.service.gov.uk/government/ uploads/system/uploads/attachment_data/file/656593/Special_ guardianship_statutory_guidance.pdf

Department for Education (2017b) *Safeguarding Strategy: Unaccompanied asylum-seeking and refugee children*, available at: www.gov.uk/ government/publications/safeguarding-unaccompanied-asylum-seeking-and-refugee-children

Department for Education (2018a) *Looked After Children in Foster Care: Analysis*, available at: www.gov.uk/government/publications/looked-after-children-in-foster-care-analysis

Department for Education (2018b) *Promoting the Education of Looked After Children and Previously Looked After Children: Statutory guidance for local authorities*, available at: www.gov.uk/government/publications/promoting-the-education-of-looked-after-children

Department for Education (2019a) *Children Looked After in England (including Adoption), Year Ending 31 March 2019*, available at: https://assets.publishing.service.gov.uk/government/uploads/system/uploads/attachment_data/file/850306/Children_looked_after_in_England_2019_Text.pdf

Department for Education (2019b) *Elective Home Education, Departmental guidance for local authorities*, available at: www.gov.uk/government/publications

Department for Education (2020a) *Adoption as a Permanence Option*, available at: www.gov.uk/government/news/councils-urged-to-prioritise-adoption

Department for Education (2020b) *Official Statistics: Children & family social work workforce in England, year ending 30 September 2019*, available at: https://assets.publishing.service.gov.uk

Devaney J, Bunting L, Davidson G, Hayes D, Lazenbatt A and Spratt T (2012) *Still Vulnerable: The impact of early childhood experiences of adolescent suicide and accidental death*, Belfast: Northern Ireland Commissioner for Children and Young People, available at: www.nspcc.org.uk/globalassets/documents/research-reports/still-vulnerable-suicide-northern-ireland-report.pdf

Devaney J, Bunting L, Hayes D and Lazenbatt A (2013) *Learning into Action: An overview of learning arising from case management reviews in Northern Ireland 2003–2008*, Belfast: Queen's University Belfast

Dingwall G and Hillier T (2015) *Blamestorming, Blamemongers and Scapegoats,* Bristol: Policy Press

England and Wales High Court (Family Division) Decisions (2012) *A and S (Children) v Lancashire County Council*, available at: www.bailii.org/ew/cases/EWHC/Fam/2012/1689.html

Evans J (2019) *Key Messages from Research on Looked After Children and Child Sexual Abuse*, available at: www.csacentre.org.uk

Family Law Week (2012) *A and S v Lancs FF (2012) EWHC 1689 (Fam)*, available at: www.familylawweek.co.uk

Family Law Week (2018) *Herefordshire Council v AB (2018) EWFC 10*, available at: www.familylaw.co.uk

Foster D and Danechi S (2019) *Home Education in England. Briefing Paper No. 5108*, House of Commons Library, available at: https://commonslibrary.parliament.uk/research-briefings/sn05108/

Frederick J, Devaney J and Alisic E (2019) 'Homicides and maltreatment-related deaths of disabled children: a systematic review', *Child Abuse Review*, 28, pp.321–338

Frost L (2019) *Blame and Shame in Social Work is not just about Media Headlines*, available at: www.communitycare.co.uk

Gladwell M (2019) *Talking to Strangers: What we should know about the people we don't know*, London: Allen Lane

Gordon A and Graham K (2016) *The National Independent Visitor Data Report, Barnardo's*, available at: www.basw.co.uk/system/files/resources/basw_50915-4_0.pdf

Green C (2019) *Co-operative Working in Safeguarding and Promoting the Welfare of Children*, Sussex: Careknowledge, Pavilion Publishing and Media

Harwin J, Alrouh B, Palmer M, Broadhurst K and Swift S (2015) *A National Study of the Usage of Supervision Orders and Special Guardianship Over Time (2007–2016) Briefing Paper no 1: Special guardianship orders*, available at: www.nuffieldfoundation.org

Harwin J, Alrouh B, Golding L, McQuarrie T, Broadburst K and Cusworth L (2019) *The Contribution of Supervision Orders and Special Guardianship to Children's Lives and Family Justice*, London: Centre for Child & Family Justice Research, Lancaster University, available at: www.cfj-lancaster.org.uk

HM Government (2005) *The Children (Private Arrangements for Fostering) Regulations 2005*, available at: www.legislation.gov.uk

HM Government (2010a) *The Children Act 1989 Guidance and Regulations Volume 2: Care planning, placement and case review*, available at: www.gov.uk/government/publications/children-act-1989-care-planning-placement-and-case-review

HM Government (2010b) *Working Together to Safeguard Children*, London: DCSF

HM Government (2011) *The Children Act 1989 Guidance and Regulations Volume 4: Fostering services*, available using the Ref: DfE-00023-2011 at: http://publications.education.gov.uk/

HM Government (2013) *The Adoption Agencies (Miscellaneous Amendments) Regulations*, available at: www.legislation.gov.uk

HM Government (2018) *Working Together to Safeguard Children: Statutory guidance on inter-agency working to safeguard and promote the welfare of children*, available at: www.gov.uk/government/publications/working-together-to-safeguard-children--2

HMICFRS (2015) *In Harm's Way: The role of the police in keeping children safe*, available at: www.justiceinspectorates.gov.uk/hmic

Home Office (2019) *Children's Asylum Claims*, available at: https://assets.publishing.service.gov.uk/government/uploads/system/uploads/attachment_data/file/825735/children_s-asylum-claims-v3.0ext.pdf

Honeyman M, Dunn P and McKenna H (2016) *A Digital NHS? An introduction to the digital agenda and plans for implementation*, available at: www.kingsfund.org.uk/sites/default/files/field/field_publication_file/A_digital_NHS_Kings_Fund_Sep_2016.pdf

House of Commons Housing, Communities and Local Government Committee (2019) *Funding of Local Authorities' Children's Services*, available at: www.parliament.uk/pa/cm2017/cmselect/cmcomloc/1638/1638.pdf

House of Commons Library (2016) *A Paperless NHS: Electronic health records*, Briefing Paper No. 07572, available at: https://researchbriefings.parliament.uk

Independent Inquiry into Child Sexual Abuse (2019) *Children in the Care of the Nottinghamshire Councils Investigative Report, July 2019*, available at: www.iicsa.org.uk/document/children-care-nottinghamshire-councils-investigation-report-31-july-2019

Jelicic H, Hart D, La Valle I with Fauth R, Gill C and Shaw SC (2013) *The Role of Independent Reviewing Officers (IROs) in England: Findings from a national survey*, London: National Children's Bureau

Jones R (2019) *In Whose Interest? The privatisation of child protection and social work*, Bristol: Policy Press

Kelly B, Dowling S and Winter K (2012) *Disabled Children and Young People who are Looked After: A literature review*, available at: www.researchgate.net

Kersley H and Estep B (2014) *Relationships for Children in Care: The value of mentoring and befriending*, New Economics Foundation, available at: https://b.3cdn.net/nefoundation//ff6e91d7f5a3ca8a7d_ccm6ba7cj.pdf

Lawson K and Cann R (2019) *State of the Nation's Foster Care: Full report*, London: The Fostering Network, available at: thefosteringnetwork.org.uk

Lord J and Cullen D (2016) *Effective Adoption Panels*, London: CoramBAAF

McIntosh C (ed) (2013) *The Cambridge Advanced Learner's Dictionary* (4th edn), Cambridge: Cambridge University Press

Morrison M (2018) *Effective Adoption and Fostering Panels in Scotland*, London: CoramBAAF

Narey M and Owers M (2018) *Foster Care in England: A review for the Department for Education*, available at: https://assets.publishing. service.gov.uk/government/uploads/system/uploads/attachment_data/ file/679320/Foster_Care_in_England_Review.pdf

National Association of Independent Reviewing Officers (2016) *An IRO Toolkit*, available at: www.nairo.org.uk/wp-content/uploads/2017/04/ Consolidated-Toolkit-January-2016.pdf

NHS (2019) *Overview: Fabricated or induced illness*, available at: www.nhs.uk

NSPCC (2013) *Child Sexual Abuse*, available at: www.nspcc.org.uk/ globalassets/documents/information-service/research-briefing-child-sexual-abuse1.pdf

NSPCC (2019) *Case Review Process in UK Nations*, London: NSPCC

Ofsted (2018) *Fostering in England 2016 to 2017: Main findings*, available at: www.gov.uk/government/publications/fostering-in-england-1-april-2017-to-31-march-2018/fostering-in-england-2017-to-2018-main-findings

Ofsted (2020) *Fostering in England 2018 to 2019: Main findings*, available at: www.gov.uk/government/publications/fostering-in-england-1-april-2018-to-31-march-2019/fostering-in-england-2018-to-2019-main-findings

Parker R (1999) 'The shaping of child care policy and practice: past and future', in Holman B, Parker R and Utting W, *Reshaping Child Care Practice*, London: National Institute for Social Work

Perraudin F (2019) 'Councils spend millions on agency social workers amid recruiting crisis', *The Guardian*, 8 April

Reder P, Duncan S and Gray M (1993) *Beyond Blame, Child Abuse Tragedies*, London: Routledge

Reder P, Duncan S and Gray M (2009) *Beyond Blame, Child Abuse Tragedies Revisited*, London: Routledge

Robertson A, Cresswell K, Takian A, Petrakaki D, Crowe S, Cornford T, Barber N, Avery A, Fernando D, Jackin A, Prescott R, Klecun E, Paton J, Lichtner V, Quinn C, Ali M, Morrison Z, Jani Y, Waring J, Marsden K and Sheikh A (2010) 'Implementation and adoption of nationwide electronic health records in secondary care in England: qualitative analysis of interim results from a prospective national evaluation', *British Medical Journal*, BMJ 2010; 341:c4564

Rose W and Barnes J (2008) *Improving Safeguarding Practice*, London: DCSF

Rothwell C, Kehoe A, Farook S and Illing J (2019) *The Characteristics of Effective Clinical and Peer Supervision in the Workplace: A rapid evidence review*, available at: www.hcpc-uk.org/resources/reports/2019/effective-clinical-and-peer-supervision-report/

Selwyn J, Wijedasa D and Meakings S (2015) *Beyond the Adoption Order: Challenges, interventions and adoption disruptions*, London: CoramBAAF

Sesar K, Simic N and Barisic M (2010) 'Multi-type childhood abuse, strategies of coping, and psychological adaptations in young adults', *Croatian Medical Journal*, 51:5, pp.406–416, available at: www.ncbi.nlm.nih.gov/pmc/articles/PMC2969135

Sheridan MS (2003) 'The deceit continues: An updated literature review of Munchausen Syndrome by Proxy', *Child Abuse & Neglect*, 27:4, pp.431–51

Sidebotham P, Brandon M, Bailey S, Belderson P, Dodsworth J, Garstang J, Harrison E, Retzer A and Sorensen P (2016) *Pathways to Harm, Pathways to Protection: A triennial analysis of serious case reviews 2011 to 2014*, available at: https://assets.publishing.service.gov.uk/government/uploads/system/uploads/attachment_data/file/533826/Triennial_Analysis_of_SCRs_2011-2014_-Pathways_to_harm_and_protection.pdf

Simmonds J (2011) *The Role of Special Guardianship: Best practice in permanency planning for children (England and Wales)*, London: BAAF

Simmonds J, Harwin J, Brown R and Broadhurst K (2019) *Special Guardianship: A review of the evidence. Summary report*, Nuffield Family Justice Observatory, available at: www.nuffieldfjo.org.uk/files/documents/NuffieldFJO-Special-Guardianship-190731-WEB-final.pdf

Social Work England (2019) *Professional Standards Guidance* (last updated 31 July), available at: www.socialworkengland.org.uk

Sullivan PM and Knutson JF (2000*)* 'Maltreatment and disabilities: a population-based epidemiological study', *Child Abuse & Neglect*, 24:10, pp.1257–73

Sullivan J and Quayle E (2012) 'Manipulative styles of abusers who work with children', in Erooga M (ed) *Creating Safer Organisations: Practical steps to prevent the abuse of children by those working with them*, West Sussex: John Wiley & Sons

Taylor J, Stalker K and Stewart A (2016) 'Disabled children and the child protection system: a cause for concern', *Child Abuse Review*, 25:1, pp.60–74

The Fostering Network (2018) *Foster Care in England: A review for the Department for Education by Martin Narey and Mark Owers. Response from The Fostering Network, April 2018*, available at:

www.thefosteringnetwork.org.uk/sites/www.fostering.net/files/content/tfnresponsetofosteringstocktakefinalapril18.pdf

The Fostering Network (2019) *Fostering Statistics*, available at: www.thefosteringnetwork.org.uk/

Thomas C (2018) *Care Crisis Review: Factors contributing to national increases in numbers of looked after children and applications for care orders,* London: Family Rights Group, available at: www.frg.org.uk

Timpson E (2019) *Review of School Exclusion*, available at: https://assets.publishing.service.gov.uk/government/uploads/system/uploads/attachment_data/file/807862/Timpson_review.pdf

UK Statutory Instruments (2005) *The Special Guardianship Regulations 2005*, available at: www.legislation.gov.uk

United Nations Convention on the Rights of the Child (1990) *Convention on the Rights of the Child*, London: UNICEF UK, available at: www.unicef.org.uk

Vincent S (2010) *Learning from Child Deaths and Serious Abuse*, Edinburgh: Dunedin Academic Press

Vincent S and Petch A (2012) *Audit and Analysis of Significant Case Reviews*, Edinburgh: Scottish Government

Wells K (2019) 'I'm here as a social worker': a qualitative study of immigration status issues and safeguarding children in private fostering arrangements in the UK', *Child Abuse Review*, 28, pp.273–286

Youth Justice Board (2015) *Youth Offending Teams: Making a difference for children and young people, victims and communities*, available at: https://assets.publishing.service.gov.uk/government/uploads/system/uploads/attachment_data/file/445271/Board_Visits_Final_Report.pdf

Legislation

Adoption and Children Act 2002, available at: www.legislation.gov.uk

Children Act 1948, London, HMSO, available at: www.educationengland.org.uk

Children Act 1989, London: HMSO, available at: www.legislation.gov.uk

Children Act 2004, London: HMSO, available at: www.legislation.gov.uk

Children and Families Act 2014, London: The Stationery Office.

Local Authority Social Services Act 1970, London: HMSO, available at: www.legislation.gov.uk

The Fostering Services (England) Regulations 2011, available at: www.legislation.gov.uk